JESUS IN ACTION

OTHER BOOKS BY DR. ROBINSON

JESUS IN ACTION

by

Benjamin W. Robinson

PROFESSOR OF NEW TESTAMENT INTERPRETATION
IN THE CHICAGO THEOLOGICAL SEMINARY

New York

THE MACMILLAN COMPANY

1942

PREFACE

THE religion of Jesus spread through the Roman Empire and finally around the world because it contained from its very beginning an inherent life and appeal. It is to study this active spirit, this living quality, this growing edge, that the present volume is written. May these pages open the way to a vision of the forward trail, the higher climb, the pioneering, creative spirit of our religion.

Jesus is the center of our interest. This does not mean that every saying quoted was necessarily spoken by Jesus personally. Often statements and sayings of his followers are quoted when they show the spirit of his life and message. It is the gospel which went out from Jesus to save the world which is our subject of study. Some readers may be disturbed by an impression that the author is trying to prove something, or that he is following the proof-text method and that the argument is labored. The purpose of this volume is rather to linger a while with Jesus, to converse with him, to become acquainted with his healthy spirit.

It is hoped that there is nothing sectarian in this book. It is written for Christians and modern thinkers of whatever creed or church. We are all pilgrims seeking a country. Comparisons between Jesus and others are not meant to be odious. There is no thought of hinting at the inferiority of the others, but only at the genius of Jesus. If admirers of Socrates or of Moses will understand that the author shares their profound admiration, we can still be friends. If the reader will take a "positive" attitude toward these pages he may find much of interest. Hold on to what is good and forget the rest.

These chapters represent the studies of a lifetime. If in some cases the chapters show independence of each other, it is because they were originally written for different occasions or separate publication. The first to be published many years ago was under the title, "Forcefulness in the Comparisons of Jesus" (Journal of Biblical Literature, Volume xxiii). Part of Chapter X was published in The Chicago Theological Seminary Register, 1930, under the title, "The Distinctive Quality in the Religion of Jesus." Other parts are given in substance in Chapters XIV and XV of my *Sayings of Jesus* (Harper's, 1930), which also contains my translation of the Sayings. My interest in this subject reaches so far back into my youth that I feel I must have absorbed it originally from the sermons of my father, Willard H. Robinson. In going through his notes after his death I found a large amount of material on the subject. Most of the quotations from Browning, Shakespeare and other English Classics I owe to him. I have spent much time in selecting and editing the most usable of his notes. Critics will easily distinguish between the older and the younger. Friends of Jesus will try to find in both alike a way of closer companionship with him.

My special thanks are due to my good friend, Seido Ogawa, pastor of the Paia Congregational Church of Maui, Hawaii, who has read the manuscript and made many helpful suggestions.

B. W. R.

Religious Humanism

CONTENTS

Part I. The Positive Personality

ix

PART I

THE POSITIVE PERSONALITY

CHAPTER I

Personal Qualities

THE personal ways and habits of Jesus reflect his character. They were free, hearty, and forceful. His manner of comparing his life with that of John the Baptist points a contrast. Jesus was not ascetic, socially cautious, or even diplomatic. He "came eating and drinking." He attended a wedding and helped in the merrymaking. When his critics sought to rule and restrict his ways, he chose to compare his life to a wedding festival where the force of freedom had fullest play. He allowed women, from whom other prophets shrank, to touch him. He was willing to tell the story of a shrewd steward without stopping to denounce him for keeping two sets of books, or the story of a selfish judge who gave a just decision only to get rid of a woman's nagging. He does not stop to condemn the robbers who wounded and stripped the Jericho traveler. A passionate and powerful purity needs no embroidery of prudery. Its pattern is woven in the fabric.

There is even a certain physical force which animates Jesus' way of healing people. Matthew, indeed, says that Jesus touched the hand of Simon's wife's mother and she arose. But Mark's older account says he took her by the hand and raised her up.[1] Almost everywhere, in fact, the Gospel of Mark betrays to us the physical energy and force of Jesus' personal ways. Not when it was day, but a great while before day, did he rise and go into a desert place for prayer.[2] His itinerant energy is pictured not by the tamer statement that he was preaching in the synagogues of Galilee but by the forceful assertion that he went throughout all Galilee preaching and casting out demons.[3] What a vivid picture of personal action is painted by the remark that he thrust his fingers into the deaf man's ears and spat and touched his tongue and said, "Be opened!"[4] What an indication of power in his eye lies behind the fourth evangelist's statement that when Jesus spoke to the arresting officers they went backward and fell to the ground.[5] Throughout the Gospels there are constant traces, sometimes subtle, and sometimes sharp, of great power and continuous movement in the physical ways of Jesus.[6]

Two instances we have of the *ipsissima Verba* of Jesus. English is not Greek, and Greek is not Aramaic. But out of the active ministry of Jesus we do have two phrases of his own: "Talitha Cumi" and "Ephphatha."[7] These two sayings of his were voiced in a tone so unforgettable that no translation could render their quality. We have them as he gave them, and they are words of strident power. No doubt there was tenderness in the tone of these phrases and in one of them the sadness

---

[1] Mark 1:31; Matt. 8:15.   [2] Mark 1:35; Luke 4:42.
[3] Mark 1:39.   [4] Mark 7:33.   [5] John 18:6.
[6] See Bruce Barton's *A Young Man's Jesus.*   [7] Mark 5:41; 7:34.

of sighing. But they were essentially words of positive and forthgoing power and as such though found only in the earlier Gospel of Mark they strike the thorough-going keynote of Jesus' ministry.

The *emotions* of Jesus were profound and powerful. John speaks of him as weeping, groaning in the spirit, and being troubled over the death of Lazarus.[8] Yet the tears and the visible shudder of that grief scarcely exceed the strong sobbing over Jerusalem attributed to him by the other Gospels.[9] Jesus' emotions, however, always had an affirmative or active aspect. He did not turn his face to the wall and weep like Hezekiah. His sense of failure and indignation never crushed him down under any juniper tree with the despair that desires death rather than life. Even while he was groaning in himself he was coming with purposeful power to the tomb of Lazarus.[10] Even as he sighed over the deaf man he said, "Be opened."[11] The fulness of his compassion for the multitude does not interfere with his healing their sick[12] or with his feeding them in the desert.[13] His surging emotion over Jerusalem does not break the continuity of the triumphal entry. Jesus was moved with compassion in direct connection with his exertions of power.[14] His conscious emotions, as we see them reflected in his life, are not something which he overcame with a vast struggle before he proceeded to action. They are rather a quality of his activity itself.

---

8 John 11:33-38.   9 Luke 19:41.   10 John 11:38.
11 Mark 7:34.   12 Matt. 14:14.   13 Mark 8:2-9.
14 Mark 1:31, cf. Matt. 8:3 and Luke 5:13.

The *affirmative* bearing of Jesus' emotion is reflected again and again in the Gospels. The cause of his compassion for the multitude lies in their being shepherdless and leads him to teach them many things.[15] But they had shepherds in abundance, blind guides who led them in their blindness and brought in proselytes whom they made two-fold children of hell. The people of Israel were shepherded in every way but the right way. A soul of less conscious power than Jesus would have bemoaned all this misleading, but Jesus was so conscious of the sole and active leadership of goodness which they needed that he viewed the multitude as leaderless. His compassion mirrors his quality. The same is true of his emotion over Jerusalem. He wept over her not because of her gross affirmative transgressions but because she had *not known*, had lost and missed her great opportunity. He sorrowed because she had failed to receive the spiritual power and goodness which had visited her in him. The ruling quality of Jesus' emotions betrays a soul aflame with the steady glow of holiness and love; saddened by the lack of a similar affirmative goodness in others, yet burning its way onward with undeterred activity.

In all personal and *family* relationships as in his emotional life Jesus shows a strong affirmative cast. There are several passages which exhibit this quality with great clearness. One of them recites how the mother and brethren of Jesus stood at the outside edge of the crowd that had gathered about a certain house where

---

15 Mark 6:34.

he was. They considered that he was going too far, and sought to restrain him by a private interview. They did not, indeed, take the intense view of the scribes, that he was possessed of the devil, but they felt that he was "beside himself." The matter was very personal. It touched his own family relations. But Jesus does not say, "I can *not* allow my mother and brothers to deter me from my divine mission." He turns at once to the antithetical and *positive* attitude of *active* and cooperative family love. *Family restraint is proffered to him, but he turns to family cooperation,* "Whosoever shall do the will of God the same is my brother and sister and mother." [16] The more we dwell upon the incident, the more we see the affirmative spirit of Jesus' thought, however negative the material or the situation which set it in motion.

Another passage has often been thought to involve, on the part of Jesus, a "bit of autobiography." [17] He takes up the idea of the disciples that a celibate life would be more free, easy, and independent and carries it up to the lofty and positive view of consecrated celibacy. "There are some," he says, "who have gone wifeless because they were born defective. There are some who have been unsexed for purposes of harem superintendence. Neither of these classes could help going unmarried. But there are also some who have seen a great work which they could do for God if they went wifeless. In silence for the Kingdom's sake they have made the great renunciation and plunged into the great work." What a revelation of the absolute

---

[16] Mark 3:21, 31–35.   [17] Matt. 19:3–12.

and affirmative consecration to God and duty which perpetually lived in his soul and dictated his affirmative ways of thought! If by those "that made themselves eunuchs for the Kingdom of Heaven's sake" Jesus means himself, then this passage, taken with the one just cited concerning his mother and his brethren, affords us a clear and striking insight into the unvarying positiveness of his thought even when it had to deal directly and suddenly with the relationships which were most intimately personal to him.

It is hardly necessary to add that as Jesus' emotions and his personal life had a strongly affirmative cast so also the *power of his will* had an exceedingly dynamic quality. His life was driven onward by a great inward force. This power was perhaps much greater than at first sight appears, for the elements of his nature were combined into such a unity and harmony that they can only be likened to the combination of those great elemental forces of nature which together make the plastic stress that constitutes the movement of the world. He was like Wordsworth's cloud

> That heareth not the loud winds when they call
> And moveth all together if it moves at all.[18]

His peculiar energy, at least at times, made a profound impression. He was accused of being a mad demoniac.[19] He was beside himself. He was in league

---

[18] Wordsworth, *Resolution and Independence*, XI.
[19] John 10:20.

with the ruling head of the kingdom of evil.[20] These wild accusations can be understood only as distorted reflections of an actual life of great personal force. The cleansing of the temple has no doubt often been misunderstood. It was not a wild display of ungoverned anger. He did upset the tables of the money-changers who could easily have picked the money up again, but he did not set the doves free perhaps because they would have escaped altogether if he had, but simply said of them, "Take these things hence." His very passion was marked by self-control. Yet the expulsion of the traders was an act of intense affirmative energy. It was not a mere religious reformer's zeal for purifying the house of God. It was clearing the courts of the Gentiles to restore them as "a place of prayer for all nations," in order that men of every race might be free to resume their devotions there.

Jesus' love of energy and his scorn for mere words unaccompanied by power are well shown in the healing of the man with the palsy.[21] The breaking up of the tiles of the roof and the letting down of the bed was itself a sight which Jesus felt had a counterpart in his own resoluteness. He recognized how easy it was to say, "Thy sins are forgiven." The phrase did not require much exertion, but it did take power so to speak that the palsied man actually arose.

The pure power of which Jesus was conscious is also seen in his treatment of the charge that he cast

---

[20] Mark 3:21-22; Matt. 12:24; Lk. 11:15. [21] Mark 2:1-12.

out demons through Beelzebub. Jesus replies that if Satan cast out Satan his kingdom is at an end and that a house divided against itself cannot stand. His reply reflects his own consciousness of spiritual power. The kingdom of God is really here in battle's magnificently stern array. It is quite true that one evil does cast out another. Many internal antagonisms do exist in the kingdom of evil which carries within itself the very soul of disorder and anarchy. But Jesus' consciousness of direct spiritual power ignores all these in his reply, and he declares that it is by the spirit of God and the finger of God that he casts out demons and that in him the power of the kingdom of God is actually and actively present.

A soul which is conscious of its own perfect and undivided power sees no place for the divided and discordant service which is rendered by weaker souls. In the world and in the Church as we see them, men do serve both God and mammon with conspicuous success. The kingdom of hell does continue though divided against itself in many ways. But there were no such divisions in the soul of Jesus himself nor can they exist in an ideal world, and the very fact that Jesus does not recognize them is a striking proof of his consciousness of an absolute spiritual and ethical energy. Moreover Jesus was conscious not only of this total inward force but also of its going forth from his person. In the fullest and most comprehensive sense of the words "he perceived that virtue went forth from him." He felt that his force *created force in others*. When it lodged in them it began a healing and life-giving career of its own. He came that men might have "life" and have it "abundantly."

He felt the positive and affirmative power which dwelt in him to be *the spirit of God* himself. It is the positive quality, the affirmative, energetic and missionary quality of the divine spirit that interests us here. For the Holy Spirit is as varied a thing to men as the individual conceptions of it which grow out of their different thoughts and missions.

Emerson says that the teachings of the High Spirit are abstemious, and, in regard to particulars, negative. Socrates' genius did not advise him to act, but if he purposed to do something not advantageous, it dissuaded him. "What God is," he said, "I know not; what he is not I know." The Hindoos have denominated the Supreme Being, the "internal check." The illuminated Quakers explain their light, not as somewhat which leads to any action, but it appears as an obstruction to anything unfit.[22]

In Buddha, notwithstanding his missionary impulse, two negative ideas, a great renunciation of the world and a down-sinking into the cessation of desire, constituted principal rules. The most rapid glance at the Gospels shows that the spirit of God, as Jesus felt it, was precisely the reverse of all this. It came upon him at baptism. It filled him. It drove him into the wilderness, and in its power he returned into Galilee. It sent him among the children in the market-place and to the Pharisaic banquet. It led him into the full tide of so-

[22] Essay on Swedenborg.

ciety and kept him in Capernaum where roads met
and the news of the world was to be had. It made his
life so rich, so social, and so devoted that his enemies
said he lived too freely and associated with disreput-
able characters.

The dove and voice at the baptism corresponded to
inner experiences of Jesus' soul. For to such souls as
his, symbols are to experience what metaphors are to
great literature. Metaphors are not too obtrusive but
are servants to the intensity of thought. In like manner
for Jesus the dove and voice would be less rich and
vivid than the consciousness of sonship and empowerment to which they correspond. The specific words
to Jesus at the baptism moreover suggest Old Testament passages whose whole contents he knew and felt
vibrating through the brief words. The servant in
whom God delighted and upon whom he put his Spirit
is elevated to sonship. In the Isaiah passage he will
have the nations for an inheritance and the uttermost
parts of the earth for a possession, a son who will not
fail or be discouraged till he has set justice in the earth,
a son whose gentle and unstriving ministry is nevertheless so positive that he is to be not only a covenant
to Israel but a light of the Gentiles, one who will open
blind eyes and bring prisoners from their dungeons
and them that sit in darkness out of their prison-
house.[23]

The quality of the Divine Spirit of which Jesus was
conscious at his baptism must not be interpreted as a

---

[23] Isaiah 42:1–13; Psalms 2:7–12.

mystic quietude but *in the light of the missionary chapters* whose mere captions the Divine voice quoted and intensified. So read, they are an overture in Jesus' soul which indicates the symphony of progressive love and power which his active career was to compose. That we make no mistake here is clear from the fact that the first evangelist afterwards specially and fully applies one of the same chapters to Jesus as belonging to his Spirit and work.[24] There are many definitions of the Holy Spirit but the best one is that which writes after it as its equivalent a summary of the active ministry of Jesus Christ, and that ministry grew out of the outward unfolding of his baptismal consciousness, as we see it after careful reading of the words and chapters expressly connected with it.

It is important, still further, that we should realize the positive and affirmative manner in which Jesus conceived of his own *mission* at the time of baptism. John the Baptist speaks of Jesus [25] as one whose fan is in his hand and who will burn the chaff among mankind with unquenchable fire. If this description corresponded to the consciousness of Jesus himself, it would connote a very large destructive and negative element in his ministry. He would have in his hand Milton's "two-handed engine" which smites once at the root of each evil tree and smites no more. We may perhaps think of these words of the Baptist's as expressed in terms of John's own conception of the final judgment.

[24] Matt. 12:18–21. [25] Matt. 3:12.

When Jesus' work was well under way John was full of doubts, and from the gloom of his prison sent messengers to inquire whether Jesus felt himself to be the Messiah or not. Jesus was doing works of beneficence only. His ministry seemed to contain none of the destructive elements which John had prophesied and for which he looked. Where were the axe and fan and flame of judgment? With marvelous tact Jesus detained the messengers till they could see still further examples of his healing and helping and then sent them back to John with the desire that such a solely constructive ministry should not be an offense to him.

Instead of limiting the affirmative character of Jesus' consciousness by the negative characterizations coming at the outset from the mouth of the Baptist we should in the light of Jesus' message to John regard those characterizations as a dark background well suited to bring out by contrast the bright movement of Jesus' affirmative beneficence, just as old painters used to put dark scenes in the gray background of their sunny pictures of Jesus making his triumphal entry or performing some miracle of love. The procession of Jesus' activities, as he felt them forming in his soul and issuing forth, carried a banner with a new inscription, "The Son of Man came to save and fulfil, rather than to deny or destroy."

Many expressions of the Fourth Gospel are full of suggestion here. "God sent not his Son into the world to judge the world but that the world should be saved through him." [26] His aim was to keep men from perish-

---

[26] John 3:17.

ing, by giving them eternal life.[27] The thief's work of killing and destroying is not a part of the work of the Good Shepherd but an antithesis to his abundant giving of life.[28] The three brief allegories of the door, the sheep, and the Good Shepherd well portray the perpetually positive and affirmative tenderness and progressive sacrificial love of Jesus. Like his own life they contain no negative note.[29]

The conception we have been giving of the positive quality of Jesus' consciousness is confirmed by a general view of the great *spiritual crises* and struggles of his soul, his baptism, temptation, transfiguration, and triumphal entry. In none of them does he betray a break with his past life, or any great revulsion or conversion. In this respect he stands in marked contrast with Paul, whose revolutionary break-down on the Damascus road has no counterpart in the life of Jesus. Jesus did indeed join the great multitudes who were baptized by John confessing their sins, but there is no indication of anything in his life to which at that time he said the "No" which renounces sin. He had no past to crush and annihilate. Someone has likened the great ravines which lead down to the Jordan to fiords down which the souls of the multitude sailed to the billowy wilderness as to a sea. The "multitudes" were moved by the spirit of repentance and also by desire to share in the new Kingdom which was at hand. The soldier felt the guilt of his individual violence and the tax-gatherer the guilt of his illegal extortions.

[27] John 3:16.   [28] John 10:10.   [29] John 10:1-6; 7-13; 14-18.

For Jesus it was only the one bright sail of the hope of the Kingdom and of dedication to its work which was filled by the divine spirit that sent him to Jordan. He felt no "vicious quitch of blood or custom" which he needed to pluck wholly out of his soul. But he was filled with the deep purpose to plant himself afresh with the living power and to give his life for the life of Israel and of the world. He sought to fulfil all righteousness. Nor can anyone fix his mind upon the earlier sources for the account of the baptism as compared with the later ones, without feeling the remarkable force and power with which Jesus dedicated himself to this fulfilment. The heaven which his soul saw was not only "opened"; it was "rent asunder," and the dove which made its nest and rest in his soul did not lead him gently but became a dynamic thing whose spirit "drove" his spirit relentlessly on.[30]

Nor is there anything in the three temptations of Jesus to alter this impression. Not one of them, as Jesus took it, is a temptation to abandon duty or to give up his work or even to indulge in the sins of the flesh. The devil's temptations of Jesus are no counterpart to the story of St. Simeon on his pillar. Satan invited Jesus to transform stones into bread. This might seem to stand for a direct temptation to bodily appetite but that is hardly a full account of the matter. The temptation must be understood in the light of Jesus' answer that men should not live by bread only. This must be read in the light of his ministry. For the message and burden

---

[30] Cf. e.g., Mark 1:10, 12 with Matt. 3:16; 4:1.

of Jesus were "life." It was his great word. How man should *live* was his theme. Life did not consist in raiment, food, or possessions but in knowing God and in living in him. Hence Jesus does not reply, "The pangs of hunger are upon me but I would rather starve than yield." That would have been the reply to direct bodily temptation. But he is full of the thought of life. He enspheres and loses the temptation in that greater whole. "Yes, I must live by bread but not by bread alone, but also by the living word of God," thought of in old Isaiah's fashion as coming down from heaven, taking effect and doing its work as a living thing and returning to heaven filled with achievement. "I have food to eat that you know not of. There is a word of God upon which I can live and which I can give to others to be their life." [31]

Jesus is set upon the pinnacle of the temple and invited to cast himself down. But here again the temptation of Jesus is rightly understood only in the light of the Psalm which Satan quotes and of Jesus' consciousness of the nature of his coming career. His life is not to be one of exhibition and publicity. Nor does the Psalm promise any up-bearing to one who is flitting proudly along the high places of life and touching them one after another with the dainty wing of self-display. The promise is to the man who is tramping along the hard path of duty and the infested ground where the wild beasts of life lurk to destroy the soul. This temptation is not one that comes to an unem-

[31] Matt. 4:4. Cf. Isaiah 55:11 as well as Deut. 8:3.

powered soul struggling between two worlds, one dead, the other "powerless to be born." It comes to the man whose lot is chosen and his portion fixed. It concerns the direction of the main sweep of his life purpose, and the manner and spirit of it.

The third temptation in like manner is aimed at nothing negative in Jesus. He loved the world and wished to save and bless it. He felt himself to be God's own son and wished to win all men to be God's sons like himself. Satan's offer of the world and its kingdoms and their glory seems for a moment to feed this heart hunger of Jesus. Might he not win the world to be God's sons at last if for the time he would yield to their desire for an outward and selfish kingdom? Might he not eliminate the otherwise necessary cross from his own program as Peter sought at a later day to eliminate it? Peter did later, doubtless to his surprise, find himself designated as "Satan" renewing the temptation already long past, to reach Jerusalem by a wrong itinerary.[32] These three temptations of Jesus, so fragmentarily and objectively recorded in the Gospels, reveal a soul being tested not for a break-down but— a break-down being recognized as impossible—for some deflection from the straight and higher path of a Son of God.

Somewhat allied to the temptations are Jesus' special withdrawals for long and lonely prayer. But none of these seems to be concerned with any temptation to do personal wrong or merely to withdraw from the

---

[32] Matt. 16:21-23.

world. Each of them, rather, is to be interpreted in the light of what immediately succeeded it. The third evangelist tells of such a night-long communion, but the following day came the important and decisive forward step of choosing the twelve.[33] Another such occasion of mountain seclusion is recorded in Mark 6:46. Nor must we overlook the fact that the remarkable scene of the transfiguration was the sequel to a similar devotional seclusion. The transfiguration in fact was, as it were, brought on by the praying.[34] Even Gethsemane itself was succeeded by a calm empowerment, which fills us with wonder, in his meeting with Caiaphas and Pilate. It is perfectly conceivable that all these seasons of prayer might have been followed by the humble resignation which tenders its hand to the sad angel of duty. Such a conception, however, we are unable to entertain in view of the events and actions which followed them. "Not as I will, but as Thou wilt" were not the words of one hanging to a last shred of hope in a desperate act to convince himself of the path of duty. They were the words of one whose course of action was already clearly outlined. Jesus' special seasons of prayer must therefore be viewed as the mounting of a strong soul into a still higher realm of wisdom, love, and sacrifice.

Jesus was transfigured six days after declaring his purpose to go to Jerusalem and meet the cross which was confronting him.[35] Some Christians feel that the

---

[33] Luke 6:12–16. [34] Luke 9:28, 29.
[35] Mark 9:2, Luke 9:28, Matt. 17:1.

transfiguration was vouchsafed to Jesus with the especial purpose of showing that he need not have undergone the cross but might have entered into glory by a direct path then and there. The transfiguration would thus be inserted as a kind of parenthetic negation to his purpose of love and sacrifice. But often in Hebrew prophecy God is the great sufferer. His travail pangs for men, his divine and lonely agony of battle for them are qualities of God upon which Isaiah expends the passion of his poetry.[36] This thought, in a far greater purity and power than Isaiah could give it, lived in the soul of Jesus. His carrying it on through and beyond the cross was the very essence of his being. This purpose of suffering for men was glowing at its intensest climax, and his spirit was in such communion and union with God, the great Sufferer, that this moral and spiritual glory irradiated his inward being and became so powerful that it poured itself through the very tissues of his body. The transfiguration, then, was not an interrupting brilliance in set antithesis to the gathering darkness of Jesus' last days but a positive part of the mounting glory of his increasing power of action and service.

The washing of the disciples' feet [37] shows the same quality. Jesus' taking the towel and girding himself, pouring water into the basin and insisting upon washing Peter's feet, while at the same time he rebukes his extravagant request for his hands and head also, are details which reveal the even balance and the un-

---

[36] Isaiah 42:14.   [37] John 13:1–11.

pausing power of Jesus' spirit. The whole incident is sometimes given a slightly negative tone as if it read, "Jesus, although he knew that he came from God and went to God and was now fully conscious of his divine glory, did, nevertheless, condescend to wash his disciples' feet." But the Gospel gives the incident a special introduction which fixes upon the personal outflow of Jesus' love. He loved his own "to the uttermost." The washing of the feet was an illustration of this full tide of love. It was the power of the coming glory as Jesus felt it in his soul that made him redouble his tenderness toward them. The washing of the disciples' feet was an enacted object lesson. It was a natural and genuine act of service proceeding from the unutterably tender love of his soul at that hour. That is to say it was not a negative act of condescension in intrinsic *contrast* to the glory into which he was to enter but it *was* the pure glory of that heaven of love into which he was entering and in which, indeed, he was already living.

Jesus himself, then, was a highly positive personality. From the very fringe of his garment to the secret place of his soul a strange and vital force was present. A Being whom he called his Father so filled his soul that the inward fulness created an outward pressure toward love and service. In table-talk, in tone of voice, in movement of emotion, in thinking, in doing, he was invariably animated by an affirmative, forthgoing power.

CHAPTER II

Assertion of Leadership

THE positive impression which Jesus made upon his friends and observers is everywhere recognized. At the close of the Sermon on the Mount the multitude felt that he had been teaching as one that had authority.[1] Noting the effective force of his words to "unclean spirits" they said, "With authority he commands even the unclean spirits and they obey him."[2] He had power on earth to forgive sins.[3] He made the impression upon the Roman centurion of being a man in the habit of being obeyed by subordinates, even when the obedience meant making a "withered palsy cease to shake." Even the wind and the sea "obeyed" him and were "muzzled" into silence.[4] When once we begin to listen to them, the assertions are numerous and insistent. He revised the Bible of his day, "You have heard that it has been said . . . but I say unto you." His sway is universal. "All things have been delivered unto me of my father."[5] In the Fourth Gospel he is the eternal bread, the essential light, the living water. He sent word to the Baptist that it was blessed not to find

[1] Matt. 7:29.   [2] Mark 1:27.   [3] Matt. 9:2–8.   [4] Mark 4:39–41.
[5] Matt. 11:27.

any occasion of stumbling in him and declared on a memorable occasion that if acknowledgment were withheld by his disciples the stones in the roadway would become vocal in his honor.[6]

Perhaps it is not as sufficiently noticed that with equal emphasis Jesus, on the other hand, disclaims any personal authority or dignity and utterly renounces those miracles by which law-givers and prophets in Israel had asserted themselves. In vain men asked him for a sign from heaven. He would not ask the sun and moon to stand still, nor the manna to descend, nor the pillar of fire to glow. He declared that he was meek and lowly of heart. He dropped out of his speech every comparison of his kingdom to any Igdrasil tree reaching to heaven and spreading to the horizon, or to the crouching lion that cannot be disturbed or to the mountain that filled the whole earth. With wonderful charm of modesty he called his flock a little one,[7] or likened his kingdom to a mustard seed that, when grown, scarcely attained the rank of a tree or to leaven that spread through some domestic batch of meal. Quite remarkably he at one time called his immediate followers not disciples but "little ones." [8] It was entirely forgivable to speak evil words against him, a mere son of man,[9] and he had no formal and final judgment to pass upon any one.[10] He asked the rich man in Mark 10:18, "Why do you call me good?"

There is a paradox here but no self-contradiction.

---

[6] Luke 19:40. [7] Luke 12:32. [8] Matt. 10:42.
[9] Matt. 12:32; see Mark 10:18. [10] John 8:15.

Jesus' self-assertion and his self-effacement belong side by side. Just before saying that he is meek and lowly of heart he insists that all things have been delivered to him by his father and asks men to take upon themselves the yoke of obedience and service to himself.[11] Jesus, in a word, lives a life of modesty and humility, a life of self-sacrifice devoted to the unspectacular service of others and to the fearless and heroic assertion that God is a father who loves the children of men as his own sons. His self-effacement and modesty are part of the ideal life he actually lives; his self-assertion belongs to his insistence that this very life, meekness and lowliness included, is one with the life of God, that to live it is to be in union with him and that to fail of it is the one irreparable calamity. Hence Jesus affirms himself whenever the question of the necessity of this life or of its eternity and its glory, as shown in himself, is at stake. Some doubted his personal authority and commission as an individual man. He waived the point. He did not insist upon himself. But at the same time he insisted, with an affirmative and positive force to which nothing could be added, that the principle which his life embodied was as eternal as God and the continuous violation of it involved a ruin without remedy.

Nor is it difficult in some items of his biography to trace the difference between the personal and impersonal view. On one occasion his enemies said he cast the demon out of a man through collusion with the prince or commander of the whole army of demons.

---

[11] Matt. 11:27-29.

But the slanderers knew in their own souls that the accusation in this case was not true. The cure, involving both blindness and dumbness, and filling every plain and honest man with amazement, was too great for that.[12] They knew that this was no case of the king of France marching twenty thousand men up a hill and then down again. It was no "glorious victory" in which a pure-minded little Peterkin would see no good at all. They knew that such work as this, if done by Satan, would be like a commander putting his own troops to death. This was no specimen of the internal tactics of evil. It was a clear case of Jesus himself winning a direct victory through the Spirit of God himself.

Nothing could be more personal for Jesus than this issue. But his enemies discounted his personality and he therefore proceeds to separate the eternal issue involved from his own individuality. He sinks himself out of sight and asserts the impersonal and absolute element. He does not say, "If I by the spirit of God cast out demons, then it is evident that I come directly from God and work with his authority." That was the introductory night logic of Nicodemus, but Jesus does not use it. He turns to the general aspect of the case and makes not the *personal* inference but the broad and comprehensive one and says, "The kingdom of God is come upon you." [13]

He goes much further. Instead of intensifying the guilt of assaulting him after such a work, he says with

---

[12] Matt. 12:22 f.   [13] Matt. 12:28.

the greatest meekness that the attack upon him as an individual son of man may be forgiven and as such shall be. But to charge darkness with light and light with darkness, to turn evident goodness into serpentine evil, is to sin against the very spirit of holiness. Here again he puts himself still further out of sight behind the principle at stake. And lastly in a remarkable reading found only in Mark he separates from any future judgment the guilt which he has already separated from his present personality, and declares it unforgivable just because it is the guilt of "an eternal sin." Thus the unforgivableness loses its individual relation to Jesus and belongs to the unalterable nature of permanent moral fixity.[14]

Thus it was the impersonal and the eternal in himself which Jesus asserted, and when he asserted himself it was for the sake of the impersonal and eternal. The truth and the prophet were one in the last analysis. But he could separate them, because sometimes the separation was ethically and spiritually important. The Kingdom of God was at hand. Its principal functions belonged to its principal officials. Some would think that unauthorized persons must not do the work which belonged to prime ministers and grand viziers. The disciples discovered a man casting out demons. The work itself was good but the irregularity was ominous. They enjoined him to stop it. But Jesus recognized it and in his gracious way intimated that a man who could do such things in his name was right at the core

---

[14] See Matt. 12:28, 31 f.; Mark 3:29.

and that the rightness was entirely separable from any local attachment to his personality and was to be trusted and encouraged.[15] The marvelous freedom with which Jesus alternately separates his own person from the eternal verities and again identifies himself with them is explained by the varying nature and demands of his work. Sometimes the principles could get better acceptance by separating them from his person. Sometimes they gained authority by being identified with it.

At the close of his life Jesus more openly and clearly identified himself with the life and principles which he asserted. This is the meaning of the triumphal entry. The end was near and the union of eternal quality and historic personality must be clearly asserted. He therefore affirms himself openly and plainly. He insists that the stones of the pathway are in league with him. The untrained beast of the field submits to his reign. The children's hosannas pay him their natural homage and the general multitude carpet the roadway with their garments and join in his praise. The scripture is fulfilled and he is exhibited as the King of Israel.

He had long ago declared in words that he was meek and lowly, and that all things were delivered to him by the Father. But he had declined to be called the Messiah, because name and personality were not yet sufficiently united to eternal principle and quality. Now that the long struggle to pour the meaning into the personality was coming to an end, he shows him-

---

[15] Mark 9:38-40.

self in open symbol as identifying the meek and lowly one with the ideal king,[16] and immediately proceeds to offer this peculiar royalty of his not only to his Jewish followers but to the world at large by cleansing the temple and declaring it "a house of prayer for all the nations." [17]

It is true he immediately drops back again out of all such external symbolizing of royal self-assertion into his usual spiritual and ethical work. He did not assume even for the moment a Solomonic or imperial royalty but only a royalty which spelled out the visibly exact inscription for his own life and tuition. The triumphal entry was the assertion of the royalty of Jesus' own personality. It was also the assertion of the royalty and power of meekness and lowliness of heart. And it was the assertion that the two royalties are one.

We are told that Socrates claimed nothing personally while Jesus asked men to imitate him with the greatest exactness and follow him with the greatest closeness. Socrates asked men to neglect him personally. Jesus asked men to make him their ideal pattern and example. But such antitheses must be drawn with caution. For Jesus, as we have seen, could at times sink himself out of sight more fully and completely than even Socrates. As Socrates would sink himself in the interest of his intellectual method, so Jesus, if there were need, would sink himself in the interest of his spiritual ideal. The difference lies in the fact that even to the very end Socrates refused to consider himself as

---

[16] Matt. 21:5.   [17] Mark 11:17.

the embodiment of his own principles while Jesus at the end most effectively asserted his own identity with his spiritual ideal.

Socrates acted wisely for his line of endeavor. For an intellectual method and a set of intellectual principles may be isolated from their author and would be just as true if some other man were their source. This cannot be done, however, with religious life which is a movement of the whole nature, a matter of conduct, a personal influence, a moving power. As he himself depended upon his eternal Father and drew his life from him, so other men must in turn draw their life from him, the Son, and live by him. Theodore Parker was in error when he asserted that Christianity, if true at all, would be just as true if Herod or Catiline had taught it. Intellectual principles may be separated from the man who utters them and be printed anonymously. A consciously imperfect man may exhort men to follow his principles of life rather than his example or may exhort them, as Paul did, to follow his example only in so far as it agrees with the ideal he preaches. But if a man feels himself to be God's son in a deeper way he must ultimately and essentially identify his personal claims with his own teaching and demand loyalty to both.

Jesus was his own religion alive and *in action*. To assert the eternity of his ideal of life and its final triumph in the world was to assert his own eternity and final triumph. The disciples recognized that his Gospel was to be preached in all the world and that he himself, being lifted up, would draw all men unto himself.[18] The final judgment might be delivered by the word which he spoke or by himself in person.[19] Elemental forces might destroy the house on the sand, or the king himself in that day might personally say, "I never knew you. Depart from me ye that work iniquity." [20]

He himself was the cornerstone of the divine building for some and a stone of stumbling for others. But the very next sentence continues and yet transforms the figure by a reference of wholly impersonal character, for the reference in the last half of Matthew 21:44 and in Luke 20:18 to Daniel 2:34 f. cannot be mistaken. Jesus' "stone" is Daniel's mountain boulder cut out without hands, and his "scattered dust" is Daniel's chaff of the summer threshing floor which the wind carried away. Jesus does not mention the mystic growth of the stone into a great mountain filling the whole earth because he never used or adopted an image which went beyond the modesty of nature. But there can be no reasonable doubt that his condensed citation of Daniel's figure was meant to include the idea of a kingdom whose universality corresponded to that of the prophet. The startling thing in the whole connection is that the stone is the same stone whether viewed as a man or as a kingdom.

There is a somewhat similar identification between Jesus and the ultimate triumph of his Kingdom, which Luke connects with the return of the seventy. They

---

[18] Matt. 24:14; John 12:32.   [19] John 12:48; Matthew 25:31–46.
[20] Matt. 7:27 and 23.

have been casting out demons in connection with their evangelizing work and on their return give a joyful report of their remarkable control over these lieutenants and privates in the Kingdom of hell. But Jesus immediately makes known to them his own vision of the head and commander of the forces of spiritual evil suffering an inclusive, comprehensive, and decisive downcasting from Heaven. The figure has a strong impersonal cast. Satan falls like the flashing of lightning in the darkness of night. It is the proleptic universal downfall of evil which Jesus beholds. Yet it is he who beholds it and beholds it in connection with the glad triumphs of his own disciples as they preached his own Gospel. The abstract vision of Satan's ruin is, after all, identical with Jesus' own personal triumph.

Jesus and his Kingdom are one. Separated at times so that men might accept the Kingdom if his personality were a stumbling block, he nevertheless reunited them from time to time and, at the close of his career, identified them for all time. He never failed to assert one or the other with positiveness, and if on occasion he withdrew force from one it was in order to impart it to the other.

CHAPTER III

Aggressive Methods of Work

JESUS' positive personality took effect in the methods of his daily ministry. The situations were of course greatly varied. (1) Sometimes even when there was no attack upon Jesus the mere *sight* of the unhappy selfishnesses in the general conduct of men occasioned his own aggressive ethical attack. He observed the guests at a banquet scrambling deftly for the seats of honor. He painted the quick parable-picture of the socially ambitious man invited down from the chief seat which he had usurped, while the man who had taken a humble place was invited up to replace him.[1] Again, commercialized society was in evidence with its clearing house of social honors, its mutual admirations, and invitations for a purpose. Against it Jesus flung his genial but rebukeful picture of a supper where the invited guests were not the host's rich relatives or neighbors, but the poor, the maimed, the lame and the blind, a banquet whose giver would be perfectly safe from return invitations.[2]

On another occasion he seems to have felt keenly the

---

[1] Luke 14:7-11.   [2] Luke 14:12-14.

fundamental wrongness of the messianic ideal of some of the Pharisees. He attacked it with a force of questions: The Messiah is the son of David. Must the true son of David set up a triumphant military center to whose trade and commerce surrounding nations bring their tribute and pay their homage? So you Pharisees say? The great and significant principle of Messiahship cannot be genealogical descent from David or external likeness of authority and power but such a righteousness of heart as produces something far higher. Consider whether my work may not be that something and whether that may not call for your recognition and allegiance.[3] There could hardly be a more powerful assault upon the Pharisaic position. Its individual units are compacted so strongly in the Gospel report that some of them are even hidden from view. But it is an attack in force.

It would seem, too, as though the twenty-third chapter of Matthew which immediately follows represented in its material and even in its main arrangement the substance of a vivid and unified torrent of denunciatory attack which Jesus made along the whole extended line of certain conventionalized entrenchments. We may easily read it with a bitter elocution which is foreign to its heart, but it seems to represent a concentrated attack not made in reply to any direct assault of his enemies upon himself but brought on by a broad survey of their general position.[4]

Simon, the Pharisee, was saying within himself that

---

[3] Matt. 22:41-45.   [4] Matt. 23:13-39.

Jesus, if a genuine prophet, should have felt the sinfulness in the touch of the woman who anointed him. Jesus made no negative defense of his own prophetic qualifications but aimed his immortal shaft directly at the man's unforgiving spirit and its inferiority to the woman he despised.[5] When he gave his absolution to the palsied sufferer the scribes made their unspoken charge of blasphemy. Jesus did not directly defend himself against it but thrust home to them the difference between that critical use of the tongue which all men possess, and the power to help and to heal which he manifested.[6] At another time he was at table on the Sabbath day. The Pharisees were watching him. He did not wait for them to charge him with Sabbath-breaking when he had healed the man with the dropsy but said, "You save a dumb beast from a watery grave on the Sabbath and shall not I on the same day save a human being from his living watery grave?" [7]

The parable of the prodigal son is not solely an exposition of God's fatherhood but, like the parable of the lost sheep and the lost coin, is a home thrust to the hearts of men who murmured at him because he received and ate with sinners. Jesus does not directly defend his own conduct but draws pictures which show his adversaries their own unreasonableness and jealousy in contrast with the natural joy of God and man over anything recovered and saved.[8] There was more of this murmuring connected with Jesus' inviting himself

---

[5] Luke 7:36–48.   [6] Matt. 9:1–8.   [7] Luke 14:1–5.
[8] Luke 15:1–4, 25–30.

to Zaccheus' house. Here, too, the complaining was not addressed directly to Jesus, yet Jesus' word to Zaccheus in presence of the gathered company was another powerful and affirmative stroke at those who had denationalized and ostracized Zaccheus as a publican. But Jesus affirms his citizenship in the most emphatic form. "He also is a son of Abraham." [9] When the Jews persecuted Jesus and sought to kill him for Sabbath-breaking and for making God his Father, he did not discuss the nature of the Sabbath defensively or demonstrate his place as God's son but replied: "God works and I work." [10]

To the murderous atmosphere in which Jesus found himself toward the close of his life he answered in no apologetic tone but described it in the parable of the marriage feast which sets forth in the sharpest language the hardened disposition of those who were rejecting him and the doom of outer darkness which awaited them.[11] Finally, at the last supper, in dealing with Judas, Jesus does not take the attitude of wounded love and passively wait for the issue of the treachery in the coming betrayal. He takes the sop, "the dainty morsel," and gives it to Judas as a kind of last appeal to his love, and emphatically tells him to do with all possible despatch that which he intends to do.[12]

(2) Jesus also had to meet the direct and *outspoken assaults* of his adversaries. Yet he met them, not defen-

---

[9] Luke 19:1–9. [10] John 5:17. [11] Matt. 22:1–13.
[12] John 13:25–27; Mark 14:18.

sively, but by immediate counter-attacks. It is a strong testimony to the positiveness of Jesus that his sanity was so often assailed. The accusation took different forms. He was possessed of a demon. He was in league with Beelzebub. He was beside himself.[13] His enemies and even his friends and his family sought to place him under restraint. We have seen how on one occasion some Pharisees seemed to have used his family as a tool for forcing him out of his work. Messengers were sent to draw him aside out of the crowd. He might have merely waved them aside with the assurance that he was perfectly sane or have sharply refused to be interrupted. This would have been acting on the defensive. What he did do was to reach his strong arm over into the ranks of his besiegers and realign them not on the basis of blood relationship to himself or of ecclesiastical belongings but along the new line of filial relationship to his Father in Heaven.[14] On another occasion a Pharisaic deputation from the capital arraigned him because his disciples violated the tradition of the elders by not washing before eating. But Jesus did not defend his disciples but directly attacked his adversaries for violating, not the traditions of the elders, but the commandments of God, and quoted Isaiah's prophetic and proleptic description of their spiritual insincerity.

There is a striking instance of Jesus' method of counter-attack in his reply to the priests and elders who came upon him in the temple and asked him under

---

[13] John 8:48; Mark 3:22, 21. [14] Mark 3:35; Matt. 12:50.

whose authority he was proceeding with his work. He immediately turned upon them with the counter-question which impaled them upon the dilemma of their own insincerity, "Was John divinely commissioned or not?" If he was, then recall the recognition he demanded for me. But if you say "No" you lose the support not only of your own conscience which may not trouble you, but of the popular conscience also, and that loss may imperil your ecclesiastical holdings! [15] According to the first evangelist, moreover, Jesus pushed his offensive still further by likening his critics to a son who promised his father to go to work in the vineyard. By not actually going the son showed his inferiority to another son who hastily refused but afterwards repented and went. Were not the "publicans and harlots" really better than they? [16]

The question of the tribute money is also in point. Some Pharisees had degraded their own spiritual God into an invisible Caesar, whose principal rival was the Roman Tiberius. Was it lawful for the subjects of the invisible imperator to pay tribute to any Caesar, especially such a Caesar as Tiberius? A negative answer from Jesus would push him into the Roman net. An affirmative answer would compromise the sovereignty of Israel's viewless King and entangle Jesus in the meshes of scribal and popular reprobation. But Jesus does not defend himself by taking either side. He turns the issue away from himself and places it upon

[15] Matt. 21:23–27; Mark 11:27–33; Luke 20:1–8.
[16] Matt. 21:28–32.

them. God is the ruler of souls and to him must be rendered not only the temple tax but the allegiance of a love which obeys his law of worship and his law of love to mankind. That is, Jesus does not defend his own position but turns upon them with a sharp laconic thrust into their sense of the practical duty in their situation. "Render unto Caesar the things that are Caesar's and unto God the things that are God's." [17]

In all these instances we see the deep cosmic positiveness of Jesus' soul consistently reflected in every passing collision with the men of his day no matter how mean and crafty or how concentrated and critical their attack might be. Differences of critical exposition and arrangement in regard to the individual passages cannot blind us to the general fact. It emerges from the larger exegesis just as clearly as from the narrower and stricter one. Our citations are illustrative, not exhaustive. It is difficult to discover in the entire material of the Gospel narratives anything which represents Jesus in a merely defensive attitude.

(3) There are, it is true, a number of instances recorded in the Gospels in which Jesus makes a defense of himself or of his disciples. But in every instance the defense is a necessary preliminary to an attack. When the disciples, passing through the grain fields on the Sabbath day, began to pick ears and eat, the Pharisees saw in the act an infringement of the Sabbath. Jesus cites in defense of his followers David's eating of the

---

[17] Matt. 22:15–22.

sacred shew-bread when in the hour of his necessity he fled to Nob. He also refers to the fact that the work necessarily devolving upon officiating priests on the Sabbath does not really profane the holy day. These are defensive propositions. But Jesus immediately proceeds to show his critics that it was their hard and unkindly heart that gave birth to their strictures and that their condemnation of his guiltless disciples proceeded from their ignorance of the great primal principles of their own prophets who so often passionately taught that God subordinates ceremonial sacrifice to the more important desire for goodness and kindness.[18] Mark even reports Jesus as giving to his adversaries the direct and revolutionary proposition that the Sabbath was made for man and not man for the Sabbath.[19]

When he meets the question of the Sadducees as to the woman with seven successive husbands, he affirms for the resurrection a higher spiritual arena which throws the Sadducees' question out of court. In the risen life they neither marry nor are given in marriage and the question whose wife the woman would be has no standing. This part of Jesus' answer is highly interesting in the light it casts upon the coarsening effect of some of the current crude ideas, and sets off by contrast the intensely spiritual conception which Jesus had of the risen life. Yet all this is but a preliminary brushing away of the Sadducees' question to make room for a direct attack upon their ignorance of the five books of Moses.

---

[18] Matt. 12:1–8. [19] Mark 2:28.

(4) Jesus showed a similar method in meeting misguided enthusiasm. Reclining at the same table with Jesus and poetically stimulated by his picture of a philanthropic banquet given to the needy an unknown fellow banqueter exclaimed, "Blessed is he that shall eat bread in the Kingdom of God." But the friendliness and enthusiasm of the man were overridden by the materialism of his conception of the Kingdom, and Jesus firmly and affirmatively assailed his defective though kindly conceptions. "See to it," he said, for substance, "that you do not decline the felicity of the Kingdom at the very moment when you praise it. There is a worm at the very core of your desire. A certain man made a great supper. He invited many professed friends but when they actually received their invitations they all sent in their regrets. They did not really care to come." Jesus' thrust was gracious. It took the form of a parable and parable easily passes into sympathy. But the rebuke was, after all, real as if the man had said, "How glorious it would be to live in heaven!" and Jesus had instantly said, "Do you really want to go there?" [20]

At another time a certain woman whose name is equally unknown broke out in the midst of the crowd with her voice of maternal admiration, "Blessed is the mother that bore and nursed thee." It was one of those sincere and gracious adulations which sometimes turn a leader's attention from his message. But Jesus assailed the sentimentality at once. Motherhood is blessed

---

[20] Luke 14:15–21.

and the mother of the Messiah thrice blessed. But Jesus steps straight over this lower joy to the higher and more sober blessedness of a life that hears God's calls of love and duty and precipitates itself into a life of obedience to them.

(5) This everywhere positive method he extended even to his own *closest adherents*. The dividing line between Jesus' disciples and the outside world was not always sharply defined. They were often deeply infected with material ideas of the Kingdom. Even for them the doctrine of the cross was frequently clouded over by misconceptions. The rich and powerful soul of Jesus did not hesitate to be strong with these also. His faithfulness to them, though usually tender toward those who were specially his own, did nevertheless handle their misconceptions in a most affirmative temper, and sometimes when the very cross itself was at stake he attacked their misconceptions with a resolute antagonism. We have already seen how he assailed their shrinking from marriage because it imposed too strict a bond. He confronted them with the still more exacting idea of keeping unencumbered by marriage in order to make freer strides in sacrifice for the Kingdom of God. They might be unable to receive so intense a saying, but he flung it at them without hesitation.[21] When they murmured against the wastefulness of Mary's anointing, he assigned it a positive utility as if it were a part of the necessities of his burial

---

[21] Matt. 19:10–12.

and wrought it into the program of his crucifixion and the preaching of his Gospel as if it were an integral and necessary item.[22]

Perhaps the intensest instance of Jesus' assailing the misconceptions of his own disciples occurred in the neighborhood of Caesarea Philippi. It amounts to an almost personal attack. The long northward retirement has swung about into the long and last critical journey to Jerusalem and the cross. Jesus announces the tragical terminal point of his itinerary. In current messianic expectations crucifixion was a contradiction in terms. For them the first mark of divine sonship was exemption from sorrow. The good man must be the prosperous man and the perfect man must be the most prosperous of all. Something of natural affection also there may have been in Peter's taking Jesus aside and rebuking him for believing that he must suffer death at Jerusalem at the hands of his enemies.

It might have been thought that Jesus would have gently excused Peter for sharing the general conception and would have explained in some painstaking parable the necessity of the cross. As a matter of fact he turned upon him with a severity which at first sight seems better suited for assailing a Caiaphas or a Judas. A great principle was at stake as well as the exemplification of it in his own death. The incident indicates not only the supreme criticalness of the hour but the fundamental positiveness of Jesus' method even with his own disciples. He turns upon Peter and says, "Get

---

[22] Mark 14:3-9.

thee behind me, Satan." We may see in these words a reflection of the intensity of Jesus' conviction that he must meet the cross and of the great struggle which he had undergone. But it is also clear that we have here a very striking example of Jesus' general method of direct and vigorous attack upon wrong mental and spiritual positions even when they were held by his closest friends.

Nor does Jesus recede from the sharpness of his attack upon Peter. On the contrary he calls the multitude to him along with his disciples and pictures the universal principle, "You object to my taking up my cross and going to the place of execution. But look you! The whole procession of those that follow me must each one likewise shoulder his cross and be traveling with me to his place of execution in his Jerusalem." [23] The whole picture is in line with the method of Jesus which declined the defensive except for the briefest and most necessary preliminary moment and plunged at once with whatever variation the occasion demanded into an offensive onset.

(6) The fiery expulsion of the traders from the temple was not a sudden, unpremeditated act, for Mark reminds us of the preparatory survey of the day before.[24] At one time Herod tried to frighten Jesus out of Galilee. The odium of John's murder was resting upon him. He did not desire the added credit of killing a second prophet. Some of the Pharisees were

---

[23] Mark 8:34.   [24] Mark 11:11.

glad to cooperate by conveying a murderous threat from him to Jesus, for they wished to drive him into their own deadly net at Jerusalem. The calm tone of Jesus' reply is a striking even if peculiar instance of the *balanced serenity* with which he acted. He was not moved by the fox-like cunning of Herod's threat. He would remain in Galilee for the immediate future performing the cures that showed the power in his ministry. He was in no danger there but only at the Jewish headquarters in Judea and Jerusalem.[25]

Even when the excitement and enthusiasm were at their height round about him Jesus had a way of taking some minor step which revealed *the poise of his power*. On one occasion when the coming and going of the crowd was trenching upon the physical necessities of his disciples he dropped everything and took them away in their boat for quiet and rest.[26] The collectors at Capernaum asked for their half shekel. Jesus did not refuse the tribute but at the same time paid it with kingly dignity.[27] In the most uncompromising terms he insisted upon washing Peter's feet. The apostle must submit or pay the price in utter alienation. Yet when with quick surrender the disciple included his head and hands as well as his feet, Jesus tells him with almost playful evenness that one who had already had his bath needs no washing except of his feet.[28]

We are not here considering the teaching of Jesus as such but only the affirmative nature of his character

---

[25] Luke 13:31–33.   [26] Mark 6:31–32.   [27] Matt. 17:24–27.
[28] John 13:10.

and method of work. Yet it may be proper in establishing the point in question to refer to his intellectual self-control in the midst of his most intense denunciations. The Pharisees were scrupulous about tithing even from the commonest garden herbs while at the same time they often neglected to manifest the cardinal qualities of justice and mercy. A soul of less balanced energy would have delivered his attack by saying, "Away with your hair-splitting details of duty and your finical insistence upon herbs and spices, and attend to the things that are deep and vital." But it was true of the cosmic movement of the spirit of Jesus that the very least things felt his care and the greatest were not exempt from his power. "These you ought to have done and not to have left the other undone." [29]

It was with the same strong and even hand that Jesus kept or broke the ceremonial law. He touched the lepers freely with a hand that made them clean and feared no ceremonial defilement. But when it was for the healed man's spiritual good or for some other definite purpose of his mission, he told him to go and show himself to the priest and offer the gift that Moses commanded for a testimony unto them.[30] The contrast between the Pharisee and the Publican is sharply pictured. The affirmations are strong in the case of both characters. Yet it is to be noticed that the Pharisee is not condemned, at least not in so many words. The things which the Pharisee did were not in themselves evil but in part at least commendable. It was his spirit

[29] Matt. 23:23.   [30] Mark 1:41–44.

that was wrong. Jesus' expression, therefore, does not exclude the possibility of the Pharisee being justified in some small degree. Commentators have usually said with Tertullian that the Pharisee was condemned and the Publican justified. But Jesus himself does not make this antithesis. His contrast, at least verbally, is between a larger and a smaller justification. The restraint of his utterance is remarkable as well as characteristic.

In his methods of work and ministry, then, Jesus had no habit of standing upon the defensive. When he seemed to do so it was but a preliminary necessity for assuming the offensive. Nor was he carried away by the enthusiasm either of himself or of others. He never played the part of the unbalanced fanatic. His positiveness was full of symmetry and his symmetry was always positive. The balanced sentences which are attributed to him in the Gospels are not mere instances of Hebrew parallelism. They reflect the balanced movement of his affirmative speech. The upward climb by which they mount like an airplane into the loftiest form of the conceptions with which they start, represents the constant tendency of his utterances to rise to an ever higher level.

PART II

THE POSITIVE PROGRAM

CHAPTER IV

Jesus' Life Campaign

JESUS did more than take the constant local and temporary action which we have seen growing out of his positive nature. He had a definite life campaign. There are two antithetical misconceptions of it which are to be avoided. On the one hand, his life was not a stiffly fixed program. We should not read and harmonize the Gospels into a fixed outline and then turn the completed biography into a precisely prearranged life-itinerary whose districts and dates, towns and hours, personal contacts and conflicts, deeds and discourses were itemized upon the tablets of Jesus' soul and followed out in a set program. For the touch of mechanism in any such procedure weakens the sense of the ever-present creative positiveness which was found in Jesus' soul.

On the other hand, Jesus' career did not proceed from the random play of the spiritual power within him. The track of his life is not to be mapped by marking the successive deflections and new turns caused by the various conditions and forces against which he struck. That would be to deprive his life of any and every plan of campaign. It would introduce an element

of drifting which in its turn is quite foreign to any
powerful spirit.

The truth is rather that such a perfectly positive
soul as Jesus' is so broad and deep in its vision that it
sees the future in the present, the harvest in the seed,
the development in the embryo. Jesus knew the church
of his day and its authorities. He knew its party forces
and the possible complications of them. He knew the
political powers that were and the Graeco-Roman-
Jewish authority and influence. He knew that the
gracious message of a Father's love which he felt so
richly in his own soul and the good news of a coming
Kingdom of love would attract the individual and
draw the crowd. But the authorized church of his day
by virtue of its compromise with externalism and selfish greed must soon prove to be his enemy.

The spirituality of his Kingdom moreover would
alienate many initial adherents whom it could not
assimilate. Some few choice and unspoiled souls at least
he could teach and train. He knew also the infinitely
mixed and complex social ingredients of his day. He
felt, yet further, the presence of the heavy sediment
of evil permeating the whole ecclesiastical and political mass. He knew that it would breed its deadly
germs and infect the whole bulk of his surroundings
with a destructive corruption which would ultimately
slay him and destroy those who were nearest to him.
This he felt to be the necessary result of the affirmative
power of his own spiritual ministry. The Fourth Gospel
contains a passage which we may use as an illustration.
Jesus, threatened once with stoning, told his adver-

saries that he had done many works of beneficence among them and ironically asked for which of them he was to be stoned.[1] Jesus' irony is remarkable because it usually consists in a statement which in itself is strictly true. "They that are whole do not need a physician but only they that are sick." "I am come not to call the righteous but sinners to repentance." So it actually was for his good works, that is, because of the power and positiveness of them, that he was put to death.

Wherever a man of great spiritual force ministers in the midst of unspiritual selfishness, and refuses to use his power to destroy his enemies or save himself, his days are numbered. The particular form of his destruction varies with epoch and environment. But he will be destroyed. Evil men hate him, for he is their opposite. They recognize his influence and see it enhanced by words and works of great power. In clashing with him, in spite of their initial awe of him, they discover by rapid degrees that he will not slay them or destroy or even hurt them at all by brute force. Being themselves altogether ready to use such force, they have the issue in their own hands. He has a Kingdom but neither he nor his servants will fight that he be not taken. His enemies can kill him, and he will not resist. When some exceptional or mighty act of love comes, it seals his doom. If he is left alone everybody will believe on him. The movement in his favor must be extinguished by swift and radical means. Put him and the proof of his power out of sight. Kill him and

[1] John 10:32.

kill any Lazarus who is an object lesson of his peculiar abilities. "Many good works have I shown you from my Father. For which of those works do you stone me?" "They took counsel also how they might put Lazarus to death." Jesus understood this terrible logic of events.

So powerful and positive a soul as Jesus' could, moreover, see in advance the principal features and sequences in his life work. Paul probably knew from the Damascus hour the main outlines of his new religion and of his missionary career. He knew the Jewish spirit and the Graeco-Roman world of his day and he knew what had happened to Jesus. But Paul's career was more extended in geographical distance, and his soul was clouded at times by the mists that arose from his own struggles. Jesus on the contrary confined his mission to his own small land, and the natural insight of his unclouded soul was greater than Paul's. A field glass of high power applied to a limited landscape reveals the necessary course of him who travels it with a clearness out of all proportion to that which a glass of lesser power applied to a vastly greater area can possibly show. The swift and richly endowed soul of Paul might indeed foresee much of his future career. The Holy Spirit in Paul could testify in every city that bonds and affliction awaited him. Yet he could not know just what would happen to him in Jerusalem.[2]

With Jesus it was different. The lost sheep of the house of Israel to whom he was sent lived within a

[2] Romans 15:31; Acts 20:22, 23.

very limited area. Persecuted in one city he might and did flee to another but that method would soon reach its limits unless he fled from his work altogether. His specific enemies were present everywhere or could be sent after him. Everything tended toward crystallization. The time must come at last when if he were a faithful witness and would push his work forward he must turn southward again from any northern retirement and make the necessary southward journey to Jerusalem. The general necessities of such a positive spiritual career as his within such a limited area were evident. Their necessary sequence was also largely evident. The final detail of death and the manner of it were perhaps also clear. To see these necessary sequences was, for Jesus, to turn them at once into a plan of aggressive and unfaltering campaign.

There are many indications in the Gospels that Jesus had such a definite plan of campaign for his life, and many suggestions as to the nature of the plan, its scope, and its results.

1. There are frequent suggestions of system and order in Jesus' conduct of things. He did not feed the multitude until their random numbers had been reduced to symmetrical companies [3] between which the disciples could conveniently pass. He prearranged the place and details for the last supper [4] and for the triumphal entry.[5] His message to Herod, speaking as it does of performing cures today and tomorrow and

---

[3] Mark 6:39, 40. [4] Mark 14:13-16. [5] Mark 11:1-7.

being perfected the third day, gives the impression of order and planning.[6] That he intended to gather and train a special nucleus of men is clear from his careful and prayerful selection of twelve disciples. It is suggestive of a still wider system that he appoints and sends out seventy, or seventy-two, men to do a preparatory work in every city and place which he was about to visit.[7] Nor should we forget the impression he made, as of a commanding general, upon the Roman centurion who seems to have regarded him as a superior officer engaged in giving positive orders through which various enterprises were to be executed. The swift movement of the entire gospel of Mark has often been noticed. The story with its constantly recurring "straightway" seems out of breath in its efforts to keep up with the march of a great hero. Doubtless Jesus likened the progress of his own work to the spread of a conflagration,[8] and John, the fore-runner, declared that his followers also should be baptized with fire.[9]

Jesus' campaign was that of preparing for the Kingdom of God.[10] For however simple and spiritual the kingdom may be in its ultimate essence the very phrase suggests an orderly, outworking, and progressive program. When Jesus tells his disciples not to enter any Samaritan city it connotes but concentration of effort, just as when at another time he instructs them not to go from house to house while they are working in a single city but to make their headquarters in one home.

---

[6] Luke 13:32, 33.   [7] Luke 10:1.   [8] Luke 12:49.
[9] Matt. 3:11.   [10] Luke 11:20.

It was on such evangelizing expeditions rather than in general that they were taught to be "wise as serpents and harmless as doves." [11] It was not in the still air of some secluded retreat that they were to depend upon the spirit of their Father to give them utterance but in the critical and anxious places of their mission.[12] It is not for giving a cup of cold water to humble or newly-made disciples in general that the reward is promised, according to Matthew, but for giving it to the messengers of the gospel when they were out upon their circuits.[13] It is not in regard to men in an upper chamber but to men upon the road that these and many other instructions are given. They are for the benefit of those who are engaged in a campaign of missionary work under Jesus' direction.

The Fourth Gospel catches this spirit of a life campaign. Jesus is introduced as one who has a definite and divine commission and at the close of his life he is represented as having accomplished the work which had been given him to do.[14] The personal work upon Nicodemus is merged and continued in the general work for the world. In Jesus' dealing with the woman of Samaria the description passes into a missionary work which she undertakes with her fellow-townsmen, and a recognition on the part of the Samaritans that Jesus is the Savior of the world. A similar progress marks the story of Jesus' ministry to the man cured at Bethesda [15] where Jesus' dealing with the individual

---

[11] Matt. 10:16. [12] Matt. 10:19-20. [13] Matt. 10:42.
[14] John 17:4. [15] John 5:1-29.

passes into a general discussion of his ministry and of the resurrection of the dead. The case of the man born blind is developed until Jesus reveals himself as the Light of the World.[16] It then passes on to the general work and ministry of Jesus. These chapters furnish the strong suggestion of a total spiritual campaign beginning with an individual, enlarging into a ministry to the whole Jewish people, and then broadening out into a work of world-wide scope.

2. Jesus' life work among his people could be an outward failure and yet from the viewpoint of spiritual power be the complete and successful carrying out of a campaign. The Jews' search for Jesus was successfully carried out. They did "find" him. They accomplished their purpose and put him out of the way. But from Jesus' point of view they failed. They never "found" him, never grasped him, never broke down his work or even checked the accomplishment of it. He "finished" it and was glorified in its close,[17] while their own work was an increasingly disastrous success and culminated in suicidal victory when by killing the prince of life they transformed him into an immortal and all-quickening spirit, and slew themselves in doing so. Even while they were condemning and killing him they were failing to find him or hurt him and were in reality lifting him up to be a universal magnet of souls.[18]

3. The spiritual element in Jesus' plan of campaign, being the strongest, naturally controlled its outward

---

[16] John 9:37. [17] John 17:4 f. [18] John 12:32 f.

scope. Extension of area is ordinarily at the expense of local intensity. Jesus' first care was for quality rather than quantity, for the intensive rather than the extensive. The parable of the good Samaritan is in point. The lawyer inquired concerning the area covered by the word "neighbor." Jesus told him the story which showed what it really meant to play the neighbor in full to anybody. He himself limited his mission to his own Jewish people. He preferred a Palestinian intensity to a cosmopolitan diffusion. It was better for the ultimate spread of the gospel. But wherever anyone of alien race showed spiritual power in sympathy with and kindred to his own, Jesus widened his national plan to take that person in.

In his northward excursion he came upon a Syro-Phoenician woman or rather she came upon him. She sought a cure for her sick daughter. Jesus gave her not a syllable in answer. The disciples desired him to rid them of her persistent crying after them. Jesus himself asserted the national restriction of his own work. The Jews were God's children. His ministry was their bread. It was not fitting that he should take anything from their loaf and give it to the dogs just because they were standing around. But the woman insisted that dogs under a table do get the crumbs that fall to the floor. The incident has often been used to exploit some supposed narrowness or bigotry or even unsympathetic hardness in Jesus. The fact that he actually did heal the woman's daughter and the general fact that no one of outside nationality is anywhere recorded as having appealed to him in vain is quite sufficient to silence such criticisms.

The important fact to note is that it was the spiritual power of the woman's faith that conquered. Jesus was educating his disciples in the direction of absolute faith in the loving fatherhood of God. He was forever fighting to advance men along that line and he could show the essential value of such faith in no more effective way than by bringing out fully the natural and necessary restriction of his ministry and letting it be broken down completely by the power of unprivileged and unaided faith. It was Jesus' way of showing by the elimination of every other auxiliary the isolated power of that faith in God for which he was battling.[19]

It would seem also that the faith of the centurion as mentioned in Matthew was used for a similar purpose. He was an outsider but was so directly in sympathy with the idea of Jesus' power as a commander-in-chief over spiritual forces as to suggest to him the vision of many such reclining at the same banquet with the Jewish patriarchs in the Kingdom of Heaven. Jesus seems to have used the centurion's faith as an object lesson to instruct his disciples. In any case the intensity of Jesus' commendation and the principle, revealed in the picture he draws, open a window into his soul and reveal the intense affirmativeness with which he was continuously conducting, at every opportunity, his deep spiritual campaign.

4. Jesus was serenely confident of the ultimate success of his work. The fact appears in a remarkable way in his parables. Whatever difficulties the seed may have

---

[19] Matt. 15:21-28; Mark 7:24-30.

encountered on stony ground or where the thorns grow, the great main acreage consists of various degrees of positive fertility which bring forth thirty, sixty, and a hundred-fold. Whoever sows the seed of the Kingdom is in alliance with eternal forces which, though he may not understand the method of their cooperation, work day and night without cessation. The harvest is sure. However small the grain of mustard seed may be at the outset, it is sure to become at last greater than all the herbs.[20] The confidence appears more resolute still in the parables of the vineyard and the marriage feast.

The parable of the vineyard in the fifth chapter of Isaiah points a contrast. Israel is a vineyard which brings forth wild grapes and is destroyed. So far as the parable goes Isaiah has no future for his people. A soul with a less serene and confident outlook than Jesus would have drawn a similarly dark parable to represent his own day, and Jesus in faithfulness to fact does draw a dark picture, but instead of stopping with the destruction of the unfaithful, Jesus' story goes on to say that the owner lets out the vineyard to other husbandmen who render him its seasonable fruits.[21]

The parable of the marriage feast draws a picture which is similarly dark. Yet the main purpose and desire of the king is to give a great banquet and when those who are invited make light of it by not coming or by coming insultingly dressed, the banquet is not sullenly or wrathfully abandoned but is furnished with abundant guests, after all.[22] Nor must we forget the

---

[20] Mark 4:8, 27, 28, 32.   [21] Matt. 21:41.   [22] Matt. 22:10.

suggestive fringe which belong to the picture of the falling stone which Jesus draws from Daniel. It not only scatters its enemies as dust but becomes a mountain which fills the whole earth.[23] It is in connection with the success of the campign of the seventy, moreover, that Jesus has his comprehensive vision of the destruction of evil.[24]

In the Gospel of Mark Jesus does not eat his final passover as a "last sad supper with his own" but rather with the bright prospect of the day when he shall drink the wine new in the Kingdom of God.[25] Not that Jesus did not recognize the whirling eddies in the onsweeping river of the Kingdom. He recognized many a local backward current here and there and even the whirlpools of strife. There is one great saying of his which shows us his recognition of the troubles incidental to the Kingdom, "Think not that I came to send peace on the earth. I came not to send peace but a sword." [26] Jesus recognized the fact that his work would awaken many an embittered conflict. Incidentally to the arousing, stimulating and bestowing of new life in individual souls there would be divisions in family, in society, and among nations. Jesus saw these indirect and undesired results of his work with such precision and clearness that he spoke as though he had directly caused them. Such forms of speech belong to souls that are intense, who feel that their life work is a far-reaching, positive, and efficient energy. What

---

[23] Matt. 21:44; Daniel 2:35. [24] Luke 10:17, 18.
[25] Mark 14:25. [26] Matt. 10:34.

we note is the confidence of success in his general work which so evidently lies back of the words. He saw the whirlpool far down the stream but he could mention it calmly because his confident eye had ever before it the general onward movement of the great river of spiritual grace as a whole.

Toward the end of each of the first three gospels occurs an eschatological chapter.[27] These chapters are related to the previous matter something as the closing discourses in the Fourth Gospel are related to the previous matter in that book. Both portray the future relations and prospects of the new Kingdom. In the earlier gospels the outlook is upon external, historical relations and prospects. In the Fourth Gospel it is upon the inner life of the church. In the earlier gospels the events are the prelude to the coming of the spiritual Kingdom of Christ. The wars and earthquakes are the beginning of travail. Something is to be born out of them.[28] The sign of the Son of Man is to appear in the heavens.[29] Believers are to be gathered together from every quarter.[30] The gospel of the Kingdom is to be preached in the whole world before the end comes.[31] But whatever the interpretation, the triumphant setting up of the new Kingdom is distinctly in view. One can hardly read the little parable of the fig tree which Mark alone reports without feeling the same bright hopefulness in it that appears in the parable of the sower and of the seed growing secretly. "Now

---

[27] Matt. 24; Mark 13; Luke 21. [28] Matt. 24:8. [29] Matt. 24:30.
[30] Mark 13:27. [31] Matt. 24:14.

from the fig tree learn her parable: when her branch is now become tender and puts forth its leaves you know that the summer is nigh." Jesus' remarkable closeness to nature makes it impossible that he should have spoken the parable except in expectation of a genuine spiritual summer at hand.

CHAPTER V

The Positiveness of the Cross

THE cross of Christ has received a negative touch from many hands. As the last crisis approached Thomas said, "The Jews will stone you if you go, but if you are resolved we will go and die with you." This has sometimes been understood as an expression of the inevitable. Jesus was bound to fall a victim to the irresistible power of his enemies. There were plenty of hiding places among the hills of Ephraim but hiding himself would have been ignoble. The angel of duty approached him in the garb of the grave. He tendered his hand and was meekly led. Was he not the meek and ready paschal lamb? Should he shrink from the hand that was to sacrifice him? He had had many struggles over the thought. The mightier his works of love and cheer the sooner his hour, the hour when the Prince of Darkness would strike his blow. When the Greeks met him in the temple he realized that a brave meeting of the cross would bring him posthumous influence. The realization precipitated an inward struggle. Even in Gethsemane it was still a question whether he should drink the cup or set it aside. All his life he had been drifting toward the cross by inevitable fate and when the end came it was merely because he was caught in the rapids and went over the edge of the cataract.

All this may serve for outline of the fate of more than one noble martyr. It does not apply to Jesus. He interwove his own positive movement toward the cross with his general spiritual campaign and made one a part of the other. There was perhaps a difference in this regard between Jesus and his disciples. They drifted in his company toward his cross because they did not understand it. He himself strode resolutely toward it because he had set his face like a flint. They stood loyally by him until he had evidently committed himself to a policy of non-resistance. They had courage enough for any practical conflict, and Peter actually handled his sword. But with such a leader physical courage was useless and simply involved them in his fate. They deserted him and fled.[1] Jesus himself on the contrary never wavered. He was not led as a lamb to the slaughter in such a sense as to keep him from being the lion of the tribe of Judah who strode tensely forward. He was not hunted out but delivered himself up.

This distinction between Jesus himself and his disciples has been immortalized by the Second Gospel. The master and the twelve were on the road going up to Jerusalem. Between him and them, however, there was a considerable interval of space. They were amazed at his rapid and resolute strides. Was he not going into the very jaws of death? Fear gripped them

---

[1] Mark 14:50.

for him and for themselves. Then he slackened his pace, let them overtake him, and told them with unflinching clearness of his death at the hands of the chief priests and the Gentiles. Nor did he spare to insert most harrowing details such as spitting and scourging.[2] There was always just such an interval between the disciples and Jesus. In the matter of his cross he was always moving resolutely forward towards it and always waiting for them to overtake him on the way. Peter might vacillate or deny and Thomas might despair, but Jesus moved to his death as steadily as the setting of the constellations.

No one can mistake his silences before the high priest or Herod or Pilate. These silences spoke in many languages, exciting the high priest to put him under oath,[3] leading Herod and his guard to brilliant mockeries,[4] and amazing the Roman governor by his apparent failure to appreciate imperial power.[5] They differ evidently and radically from the embarrassed speechlessness of the man without a wedding garment who was questioned and had nothing to say.

Nor do the shrinkings from the cross any more than the silences imply irresolution or even hesitation. They were, so to speak, automatic. The mother in the night time rushing with bare feet across burning timbers to save her child shrinks, it may be, at each step but does not really pause or hesitate. The soldier rushing at the enemy's trenches feels the spasm and twinge

---

[2] Mark 10:32–34.   [3] Matt. 26:63.   [4] Luke 23:11.
[5] John 19:10.

of a flesh wound but does not halt. Jesus' temple agony, his Gethsemane prayer, and even his agonized quotation, on the cross, of the Psalmist's inquiry why he had been left helpless, simply accent the difference between the unvaried movement of a mechanical force and the dynamic career of a living consecration.

Jesus passed through his passion with a very different conception of it from that of many around him. Women bewailed and lamented his fate. But he told them to dry their tears for him. His suffering was part of a purposed campaign. They themselves were the hapless ones upon whom blind unpurposed agonies were to fall without plan or prevention. His Jewish enemies had their program for Jesus and carried it cruelly through. He had his program of love and sacrifice, and he was carrying it through. They thought they were nailing him up on his cross in order that their plans might not be broken, but he was climbing it himself as an integral part of his plan of spiritual campaign.

Jesus in fact conducts the events of his own passion. He knows beforehand the things that are coming upon him.[6] Instead of waiting to be betrayed and arrested, he goes forth to meet the traitor.[7] He tells the officers to take him and let his associates go their way.[8] Being brought to Caiaphas and questioned as to his teaching he takes the case into his own hands and answers no direct questions but simply asserts the unconcealed

---

[6] Matt. 26:2; Mark 14:8, 18, 27; John 18:4.   [7] Mark 14:42.
[8] John 18:7–9.

publicity of his synagogue and temple utterances. He questions his questioner and instructs him as to the right method of collecting evidence. With whatever simplicity or dignity taken, his attitude was a reversal of men's ordinary awe-struck abjectness before the high priest. A servant sought to vindicate that official's position by striking Jesus but merely brought to light Jesus' unperturbed sweetness of soul and drew forth the calm question, "If I have spoken evil, bear witness of the evil, but if well why do you strike me?" [9]

He seeks to help Pilate by asking him whether he uses the word "king" in a Roman or a religious sense [10] and assures him that in the present transaction others are more guilty than he.[11] He asserts the unworldliness of his kingdom. Pilate as Pilate is really conquered by Jesus' dignified affirmativeness and seeks to release him.[12] It is the guilty complications of his position that lead him to give his tragic command.

Helpless suffering is not necessarily negative. Cranmer could not free himself from the stake and the flames when once his execution was determined. He stood there passively suffering, it may be. But his previously matured determination to have the hand that signed the recantation burn first and the power, even when bound to the stake, to withdraw that hand at any time, not only destroyed the antithesis between action and suffering so far as the hand was concerned,

---

[9] John 18:19–23.   [10] John 18:34.   [11] John 19:11.
[12] John 19:12.

but revealed a quality in his whole martyrdom which made it a positive act. In a similar, though far more extended and complete fashion, Jesus' entire passion, even though he were unable to escape after the high priest's band had seized him, becomes a series of affirmative acts of his own. Even in Perea, he moved toward the cross with a vital self-assertion from which no final physical helplessness, even if it existed, could at all detract. Such an assertion as Jesus made to Peter, after he had been seized, that he had twelve legions of angels at his disposal, if understood in the right way, reflects the power of Jesus' spirit.[13]

For a soul of such affirmative power as Jesus' the great thought-plan of going to the cross required something more than strong assertion. It must be glorified. This occurred not only at the Transfiguration [14] when the indwelling splendor of the plan and purpose of the cross broke forth into an outward radiance reflecting the inner glorification of the thought in Jesus' soul. It also is apparent on many occasions. It appears in connection with the anointing by Mary. Jesus connected her act with his burial. Mary's gift was a splendid and costly outpouring of her soul. In like manner his death was a comprehensive and glorious outpouring of the concentrated essence of his whole life career.

Paul would have God forbid that he should glory save in the cross of Christ. He was crucified with Christ. His whole life was a crucifying of his old and evil self. The cross and the accompanying resurrec-

---

[13] Matt. 26:53.   [14] See pages 19 f.

tion were the essence of his whole missionary career and of his personal experience. In a similar and yet more profound and comprehensive way Jesus himself, throughout his whole career, gloried in his own cross.

Jesus believed in his cross because, for one thing, it was the spiritual counterpart of nature's greatest thought. He loved nature as no other man has ever loved her. It was not his mission to exploit this love in poetic forms. What he might have done is easily seen from the few poetic pictures in the Sermon on the Mount. The lilies of the field were arrayed in finer texture than Solomon in his most splendid garments.[15] It was, however, the mysterious central spectacle of nature that most attracted him, the spectacle of seed falling into the ground as if it were dying and then springing up into multiplied fruitage. He made many and various parables out of this simple fact. In his Galilean ministry he used it to illustrate the progress of his gospel, the obstacles it met and the rich success of its harvests. It was not yet time to utter the further and final seed parable of his own death. It was early in his soul though it appeared in words only toward the end. "Except a grain of wheat fall into the earth and die it abideth alone. But if it die it beareth much fruit." [16] This passage in the Fourth Gospel may be regarded as expressing the point at which Jesus' life lay closest to nature's heart. If the heart of nature can be located anywhere among her manifold processes it is surely in the fact that she is forever dying and forever

---

[15] Matt. 6:28, 29.   [16] John 12:24.

being born. With the cross forever in his heart and forming the true burden of his mission he viewed nature in a positive and optimistic mood.

Jesus had one great saying which was the cross done into an aphorism, "He that loseth his life shall find it." His great burden was not simply life, but life out of death. It was his great burden because it was the expression of his cross and his cross was the message and burden of his life. The saying is found in at least six passages in the gospels.[17] No other saying occurs so often. The variety of its wording and use in the gospels seem to testify to its substantial frequency on the lips of Jesus. He universalized it into a principle: Every man must take up his cross, not bear it when laid upon him, but take it up as an affirmative principle of his life. First, Jesus' own ever-present cross, the great necessary fact and governing thought of his life. Secondly, the cross as the governing thought of every man's life. Thirdly, the cross expressed in an aphorism which made it a success and suggested a resurrection.

Jesus' special connection of the aphorism with his own cross shows that he regarded it, not as an isolated event at the close of his life, but as the expression of a principle running all through it. This attitude helps us to consider many other sayings of his in the same light, as for example when he urges men to enter into life even at the expense of losing a hand or a foot,[18] or advises the young ruler that he must give up his possessions in order to inherit eternal life.[19]

---

[17] Matt. 10:39; 16:25; Mark 8:35; Luke 9:24; 17:33; John 12:25.
[18] Matt. 18:8.   [19] Luke 18:22.

It is true that the great bulk of Jesus' parables and of his other teachings do not directly mention the cross or the aphorism of the cross. To have inserted the notion verbally at every point would have destroyed the marvelous variety of illustration and of subordinate principles which the gospels exhibit. If the cross means laying down one's life for others the principle may be translated into a thousand forms of speech and story without repeating the verbal expression which crystallizes it. We read in Matthew 16:21 that from the time when he was at Caesarea Philippi Jesus began to show his disciples the necessity of his cross. There can be little doubt that, taking the cross in its broadest and fullest meaning, Jesus wove it into his teachings as distinctly as Paul at a later time wove it into his.

Jesus' method of handling prophecy shows that he considered his sufferings and his cross an integral part of his ministry and that he taught his disciples to the same effect. He uses prophecy in a very broad and general manner. "Malachi" had prophesied that Elijah should come previous to the great day of Jehovah and should turn the hearts of the then existing generation back to the holy teachings of their ancestors.[20] Jesus says, referring to the forerunner, that Elijah had come and that his enemies had done what they pleased to him even as it had been written of him. But what was "written of him" was the general maltreatment he received at the hands of such enemies as Ahab and Jezebel.[21]

---

[20] Malachi 4:5 f.; Mark 9:12.
[21] Mark 9:13; cf. e.g. I Kings 18:17 ff., 19:1 ff.

It is in this same large way that Jesus treats prophecy concerning himself. "How is it written," he says, "of the Son of Man that he should suffer many things and be set at nought?" The reference is a very general one though perhaps it applies especially to the fifty-third chapter of Isaiah. On the road to Emmaus also, Luke records that Jesus gave the two disciples a very broad and comprehensive review of Old Testament passages concerning himself. Beginning as far back as Moses, he ran through all the prophets and interpreted the relevant passages throughout the whole body of scripture.[22] It is important to note this breadth of treatment which Jesus himself gives to prophecy for it helps us to see how he grasped the great Old Testament ideal of a suffering servant who must suffer in behalf of the Kingdom of God and how his thought of his own life involved a corresponding continuous career culminating in a shameful death. This necessity, moreover, he continually taught to his disciples and thus upon the foundation of their own scriptures built up his own spiritual campaign of teaching regarding the cross.

The positiveness and affirmativeness of Jesus' view of his cross had their counterpart in the firmness with which he required others to accept his idea. The evangelists make us see that Jesus' teaching in this matter was more than a discussion. It was an insistent inculcation. He taught it to his disciples and branded opposition to it as Satanic.[23] Sometimes he outlined it with a genial antithesis whose sharpness pierced like a

[22] Luke 24:26, 27.　[23] Mark 9:31; 8:33.

two-edged sword. The greatest man with the highest sounding name ruled over his board of governors. Each of these in his ordered turn lorded it over those that were below him. In the Kingdom of Heaven also there was a graduation of offices. The governing principle was unselfish devotion to others. When a man began to serve others unselfishly and fervently out of a pure heart he began to have rank, but above him was the man who played the slave still more fully. So the scale of decoration and glory mounted upward till it reached the man at the top who served everybody and served them best. Jesus himself came not to be ministered unto but to minister and even to carry the principle into practice so far as to give his very life as a ransom in exchange for many.[24] This was Jesus' tuition in the art of expending life in the service of others. It was his practice of the presence of God among his disciples taking effect in the culture of the cross. He was very affirmative about it.

When two of his disciples asked to be his prime ministers in the kingdom he was setting up, he did not check their ambition but tried to make them see what they ought to be asking. There was a bitter cup he had to drain. Could they drink of that? There was an immersion in sorrow. Could they bear that? They said they could. Jesus assured them that they should share his suffering but the higher positions they aimed at having, after the preliminary suffering was over, were another matter which could not be settled by royal

[24] Mark 10:42-45.

preferences. Such positions were prepared only for those who were themselves prepared for the positions. Instilling the doctrine of the cross was for Jesus almost from the outset an integral part of his life work with his disciples. But when the general necessity for himself and for his followers was merged in the actual geographic journey to Golgotha, the doctrine and the fact, the teaching and the personal movement coincided more and more till at last the journey became an object lesson in the doctrine and the final climax surpassed the faith of the disciples and led them to desert him.

The intense language which the Fourth Evangelist in his sixth chapter assigns to Jesus is startlingly positive in this connection. "Except ye eat the flesh of the Son of Man and drink his blood ye have not life in yourselves." [25] But it is no stronger in its way than the passages of the earlier Gospels we have cited. How intensely Jesus regarded himself as laying down his life for his disciples and other men may be seen at the last supper when he took the bread which was a mere incidental detail of the passover and, breaking it, made it a symbol of his sacrifice of himself and made them eat it, and when again he took the wine and made it the symbol of his shed blood, and told them all to drink of it. We saw in the last chapter how Jesus changed the developments of opposition and the negative thwartings into a positive and affirmative program of his own. In like manner he took the cross, in itself an essentially negative and destructive thing, and made it the positive

---

[25] John 6:52–56.

symbol and embodiment of his own life and of the career he demanded of others.

Jesus regarded his cross still further as an integral part of his whole spiritual campaign because it was a practical means of turning the material into the spiritual. He was positively anxious to suffer, like a mother with child, not that the agony might be over with, but for love of the child that was to be born. His suffering, seen from this viewpoint, becomes part of an agressive movement and appears not as something inflicted upon him but as an act in his campaign of love for men. He had said, "You shall seek me and shall not find me." [26] They asked if this meant that he would go to the dispersion among the Greeks and teach the Greeks. At another time they asked if his assertion that they could not come where he was going meant that he would kill himself.[27] These hostile sayings may well be travesties of things Jesus really said to the effect that he expected to meet death and through death enter into a more universal contact with the souls of mankind. Jewish perversions of his sayings were in all probability based as a rule upon utterances so great and spiritual yet so concrete that malicious minds could twist them into caricatures which nevertheless betrayed a likeness to their originals. The frequently cited incident of the application of the Greeks for an interview with him [28] carries this meaning. Emboldened, it may be, by Jesus' recent cleansing of the

[26] John 7:34.   [27] John 8:22.   [28] John 12:20.

court of the Gentiles in order to restore it as "a house of prayer for all nations," these Greeks made their epoch-making request. Jesus saw in them the first fruits of a wide-waving harvest which could be reaped only after his crucifixion.

The allegory of the Good Shepherd displays a similar integration. The members of one great flock which Jesus is to gather out of many national folds can be reached only by his laying down his life and taking it again. Jesus goes on to say that this great work is a commandment which he has received from his father. But such a commandment corresponded in the most perfect manner to an inner spiritual determination of his own to lay down his life as a means of securing the many other sheep for his flock.[29]

The triumphal entry of Jesus has a similar bearing. When he made it his doom was sealed. It was an expression of his conviction of spiritual kingship over souls. He had refused to be made a king of another kind and on other grounds.[30] But now he himself affirmatively sets up his Kingship on its true ground, the ground on which the cross stood. It was in connection with his death, moreover, that he asserted with extreme emphasis the expulsion of Satan from the earth and his own great gathering of souls to himself.[31]

There is a striking figure which expresses the idea of Jesus that his cross was a critically necessary element in building up a spiritual society. False witnesses at his

---

[29] John 10:15–18.   [30] John 18:36; cf. 6:15.
[31] John 12:31–33; Luke 10:18.

trial declared that he said he was able to destroy the temple of God and build it in three days.[32] This peculiar accusation took such strong hold upon the people at large that they flung it scornfully at him while upon the cross.[33] Jesus had, indeed, made no vain boast of any magical Satanic or Aladdin ability to make the temple structure fall into ruins and after a brief day or two rise again like an exhalation. Yet the falsity of the witness which the false witnesses bore against him probably consisted in an alteration of something he had really said. The Fourth Gospel gives us a clue.[34] Jesus on being asked about his action in cleansing the temple says in reply "Destroy this temple and in three days I will raise it up." [35] The original utterance of Jesus which lies back of the travesty of the false witnesses seems to have been a great affirmative statement. Its general character may have been something like this: "Destroy this temple that is made with hands and in three days I will build another made without hands." [36] It is as if Jesus had said: "Your unfaithful recreancy from your God is surely destroying this edifice of marble and gold. The worst part of your unfaithfulness, moreover, is your murderous hate of me and my gospel of brotherhood. Bring about the destruction of the temple edifice by destroying me the true temple of the spirit of God if you must. But my spiritual life risen from the dead will in reality build a structure of living stones, a holy community wherein God will dwell."

---

[32] Matt. 26:61; Mark 14:58.   [33] Matt. 27:40; Mark 15:29.
[34] John 2:19.   [35] John 2:19.   [36] Mark 14:58.

Jesus then did not drift toward the cross. By positive acceptance of it he converted it into an affirmative program of his own. The positive power, with which he did this, glorified the crucifixion in his soul and made it appear to him as the very essence of Messiah's career as prophesied in the Old Testament. He even converted it into his great and ruling philosophic aphorism of finding life by losing it. He gave the idea practical dominance by rigorously requiring others to accept it while at the same time he indicated its glory. It was the practical means of replacing the material by the immaterial and of building up in the world a spiritual community of believers.

PART III

POSITIVE USE OF PREVIOUS RELIGION

CHAPTER VI

His General Attitude Toward Truth

WHAT was Jesus' attitude toward current religion and life? For a soul of such singleness and unity that attitude must be marked by one great characteristic. The characteristic itself was affirmative action. He came above the horizon of the district of his ministry like a sunrise. It was like the prophetic glory of the return of the northern tribes from captivity. They had been driven out in dimness and darkness of agony into a darkness that was thicker yet. Current hopes were that their land was to be made glorious, and the shadow of death was to be turned into the shining of a great messianic light and government of peace.[1] But Jesus' descriptions of it are more accurate and vivid as well as more spiritual. The current descriptions were like our early maps of Africa. Great rivers and high mountains were known to exist, but they were sketched in early maps with an imperfect and inadequate hand because they were comparatively unexplored. Jesus is an actual traveler in the Kingdom,

---

[1] Matt. 4:13-16; Luke 1:68-79.

and he gives us a new map whose lines are definite and distinct.

Jesus viewed the truth of his gospel as a thing of life and power which would break through all artificial restrictions. It was like new wine full of a fermenting force which would burst through and destroy any unelastic container. Or it was like a piece of new cloth which if inserted in old cloth would inevitably tear itself away.[2] Jesus' ideal scribe [3] is something like a fountain. He brings out, or, like a fountain, throws forth from his inner treasure things new and old. The verb in the passage depicts a zealous readiness in imparting.

Jesus cannot think of truth as a mere static deposit in a book. It is dynamic. It must come to the surface and spring forth. The description of this fountainful quality of the ideal scribe-disciple is Jesus' observation upon a series of parables he has just delivered. The main trend of those parables represents the gospel as seed springing up under varying circumstances. The change of the figure from seed to householder enforces the idea of the voluntary pouring forth of the truth that has been gladly received and warmed into germination. Mark's comment also is similarly instructive. Truth has a forthgoing, upspringing, radiating quality. It can be hidden in the soul only as a step to manifestation.[4] This is the ultimate object of its burial or concealment in the soul. The general principle which Jesus asserts in these passages reveals

---

[2] Mark 2:21, 22.   [3] Matt. 13:51, 52.   [4] Mark 4:22.

his positive or affirmative attitude toward all truth in general.

The negative attitude of other men has often missed the positiveness of Jesus. This is evident in his use of the metaphor of salt, a figure common to Athens as well as to Jerusalem. The Jews ordinarily used the word "salt" in the bad sense as an emblem of destruction and ruin. The Dead Sea was always there to suggest such an application. Out from God's presence and his house must come a deep and pure river to sweeten the whole vastness of the Dead Sea and make it abound in living things.[5] A salt land means barrenness and desolation.[6] The site of Shechem destroyed by Abimelech was sown with salt in sign of perpetual ruin.[7] But Jesus turns from the symbolism of destruction to the homely force of domestic use. He turns, that is, from the negative to the positive. For him salt does not stand for destruction. It is not even antiseptic. He does not make the ordinary point that his disciples are to stay the corruption and moral decay of a disintegrating and decomposing world. They may have a quality which, rubbed into the world, will keep it from rotting, but Jesus does not have such a quality in mind. It is not characteristic of him to aim at arresting decay.

He thinks of salt as seasoning. It is the world's moral insipidity, its religious tastelessness, at which he aims. Attic Salt was demanded in intellectual Athens, religious salt was demanded in the Kingdom of God.

---

[5] Ezekiel 47:6–12.   [6] Deut. 29:23; Jeremiah 17:6; Zeph. 2:9.
[7] Judges 9:45.

On that hard Pagan world disgust
And secret loathing fell.
Deep weariness and sated lust
Made human life a hell.

In his cool hall, with haggard eyes,
The Roman noble lay;
He drove abroad, in furious guise,
Along the Appian way.

He made a feast, drank fierce and fast,
And crown'd his hair with flowers.
No easier nor no quicker pass'd
The impracticable hours.[8]

In the proud city of Rome and in lowly Galilee the world of his day was not only tasteless to itself but tasteless toward God. For Jesus "the point of resistance" in the world was its indifference. What Jesus complained of at Capernaum and would have complained of at Rome was that it took no heed of his message. What he sobbed over at Jerusalem was that it had no sense for the day of its visitation. There were outbreaking sins enough in Jewish and pagan cities alike. They cried to heaven. But Jesus' accusation and his agony concerned their moral stolidity and immobility, their religious blindness and lack of perception, their utter lack of moral flavor. Immoral flavor they had in abundance but Jesus left that unmentioned. Into such a world the disciples were to mix moral pungency and spiritual seasoning so that it might be palatable to itself and to God.

---

[8] M. Arnold, *Oberman Once More*, 93–104.

The less positive attitude is well indicated by the poet Shelley. According to his idea, "It is the business of the poet by certain splendid pre-calculated imaginations, either softly to disintegrate the mass of previously accumulated existence so that it shall fall into new arrangements; or sometimes to convulse, crack and rend this mass by the blast of a wholesome explosion through what was previously a chaos. The poet would *thus* be preeminently the reformer." [9] Such a work is essentially negative and destructive. Jesus sought to re-create and regenerate. He was affirmative.

There is another figure of Jesus' which is half understood and therefore misunderstood. There was an old law against adultery. It was punishable by death. Jesus sent the prohibition past the outward deed and on inward to deliver an injunction to the passions themselves in the soul. The eye is the window or lens through which the lustful image enters and depicts itself upon the retina of the mind. Therefore tear out the eye if need be that its lenses may no longer throw the evil image upon the inward screen. The hand likewise which reaches out for the unlawful caress is an instrument which must be cut off because the contagion of the caress runs inward and infects the soul. [10] How profoundly positive the meaning of this maxim-proverb really was for Jesus is easily seen when he uses it apart from any parallelism with the Mosaic code. Then the picture of the future of the man with the

---

[9] Masson, *Wordsworth, Shelley, Keats and Other Essays*, 133.
[10] Matt. 5:27–30; cf. 18:8 f.; 5:8.

amputated hand or the excised eye is changed or rather extended. Instead of merely not having his whole body cast into the Gehenna of destruction he enters into life or into the Kingdom of God. The attainment of a great positive good takes the place of escaping a great negative evil. The pure in heart "shall see God."

A powerful testimony to the affirmativeness of Jesus' general attitude toward truth and conduct is found in the fact that he regarded neutrality as an impossible attitude. If a man was not with him he was against him.[11] If he was not against him he was for him.[12] He desired his disciples also to regard men's relation to them and their work in the same uncompromising way as either favorable or unfavorable. This is remarkable in a soul of such evident gentleness and geniality as Jesus'. It appears more remarkable still when we consider the fine balance of judgment and the equipoise of soul with which he admitted the most trifling goodness in his enemies in the same breath with which he condemned them most severely.[13] It was his polarized and peculiar doctrine of the excluded middle. The world is full of men who seem to serve God and Mammon with diplomatic and complete success. But Jesus said it could not be done.

The positiveness of Jesus finds a fine foil westward in Socrates and eastward in Buddha. The long procession of events and ideas passed through the soul of Socrates, but the deity within him made no sign unless

---

[11] Matt. 12:30.   [12] Mark 9:40; Luke 9:50; 11:23.   [13] Matt. 23:23.

something was wrong. Then it raised its warning finger.[14] But the spirit which dwelt in Jesus drove him onward to the city or the country and made him pronounce unwavering judgment in favor of the outsider when he was right and against the disciple when he was wrong.[15] Socrates' attitude toward the soul was marvelously spiritual and tender and his appeal for her most earnest.[16] Yet the aspiration of the individual soul, for Socrates and Plato, is after the preservation of its own individual purity. Its maxims call for self-restraint but scarcely ever, if at all, soar into the region of commitment to a great cause. A man who is doing right may be misunderstood and suffer from ill-repute or even be put to death. It is without having been guilty of any unjust act that Plato's ideal soul is described as he suffers death. The negative goodness of the man is especially emphasized. "The Athenians have thought fit to condemn me, and accordingly I have thought it better to remain here and undergo my sentence." [17] The difference between the man who, though guilty of no outward transgression, yet undergoes his sentence, and the man whose total life-attitude is "taking up" the cross for his fellow man, sharply points the contrast between the ethics of Plato and the spirit of Jesus.

It has been said that the Greek and Roman descriptions of the future life contain every essential element in the Christian representations except one, the posi-

---

[14] Plato, Apology 31.   [15] Mark 9:39; Matt. 16:23.
[16] Plato, Phaedo 107.   [17] Phaedo 98. Republic, Bk. II, 361 f.

tiveness of assertion.[18] Jesus' certitude of the future life has always been freely recognized. But as to the whole matter Socrates says with graceful hesitation "a man of sense ought not to say, nor will I be very confident, that the description which I have given of the soul and her mansions, is exactly true but I do say, inasmuch as the soul has been shown to be immortal he may venture to think not improperly or unworthily that something of the kind is true. The venture is a glorious one. . . ." Socrates thinks that he has proved the immortality of the soul. Jesus views it with conscious axiomatic certitude. In Socrates the soul wanders through the scenes of a wonderfully elaborate and striking but confessedly doubtful topography of a purgatorial character. Jesus with unwavering simplicity commits his soul to God as his own Father, and looks to the day when he will drink the new cup with his followers in the Kingdom of God.[19]

Buddhism displays a deep search for human brotherhood. This quest has made it a missionary power in the world. But, for Buddhism, self-sacrifice was very much like a means for personal extinction. Jesus gave men a negative which ended in a positive, "He who pours out his life will find it." Buddhism gave men a negative and omitted the succeeding positive, by saying "Let a man lose his life" and saying no more. We are told that Christ has the West and Buddha the East because the western races are active and the eastern are passive. Buddhism possesses the eastern world be-

---

[18] Paul Shorey.　[19] Mark 14:25.

cause it is a religion of obedience. Christianity has the West because it is a religion of hope and progress. It is a variation of the same theme when another author tells us that Buddhism has made the East a region of passivity and despair while Christianity has made the West a region of hopeful energy and enterprising civilization. We need not here argue the resultant question as to what is cause and what is effect, whether the environment has produced the kindred religion or the religion the environment or whether both propositions are partially true. We simply point to the antithesis between the plaintive accents of the negative counsel, "Lie down and sleep and forget your sorrow," and the affirmative summons, "Take up your cross and follow me for I am carrying mine."

Jesus had a deep and positive confidence in the successful *growth* of truth. It is just because the seed is seed and the earth is what it is that agriculture is a success. Jesus' likening of the Kingdom of God to seed under various circumstances was by no means an accidental comparison. He lived near to nature's heart not for sentimental reasons but because the operations of the kingdom of nature reflected the workings of the Kingdom of God. The parable of the tares and wheat is especially illustrative here. Do not disturb things. The roots of good and evil intertwine. Let both grow together till the harvest. Do not look upon the field with despair because of the tares. The wheat will take care of itself and the separation can be made later.[20]

---

[20] Matt. 13:24 ff.

Jesus believed in *people*. He was fond of children, both the little ones that he could take in his arms [21] and those that were old enough for him to watch as they played at wedding or funeral charades in the open squares of towns,[22] the babes and sucklings that crooned the happy words they could not articulate and those who were old enough to run about the temple courts and echo the popular momentary Hosanna.[23] He advised that grown-up people should take something of the attitude of children. He appealed to human nature continually, saying, "But what think ye?" "What man of you?" "or what woman?" [24] He especially believed in human fathers and looked at the best side of them because, as the little child was his parable of man when he is right-hearted, so the child's father at his natural best was a parable of God. "What man is there of you," he said, appealing to all good fathers, "who if his son shall ask him for a loaf will give him a stone?" [25] And lest men should fail to see that he meant fatherhood at its best he put his best and most touching strength of portrayal into the story of a certain father in particular, one of whose two sons left home.

Hence also Jesus believed in souls. They could be saved. The entrance of a rich man into the new kingdom presented a case of extreme difficulty. But Jesus was unwilling to leave the disciples hopeless even in regard to them. God had additional resources with

---

[21] Luke 18:15, 16.   [22] Luke 7:32.   [23] Matt. 21:15, 16.
[24] Matt. 21:28; Luke 15:4, 8.   [25] Matt. 7:9.

men. To men it might seem impossible. "But," said Jesus looking upon his disciples impressively, "with God all things are possible." [26] The failure of his own countrymen to receive him was another sad problem. But Jesus was unwilling to regard it as anything more than exception to the general favor with which men listen to every true prophet. "A prophet is not without honor save in his country and in his own house and among his own kin." Luke and John, it is true, following our modern fashion, give the saying as an absolute negative, "No man is a prophet in his own country." But the wording of Mark and Matthew affords an instance of the fact that the earlier the source and the closer it is to Jesus himself the more emphatic and affirmative is the form of the utterance.[27]

Jesus began his Sermon on the Mount with beatitudes. The goals and rewards which he desires for souls are remarkably and richly affirmative and indicate a general attitude on his part of belief in the capacities and possibilities of souls. These utterances are instinct with joyous satisfaction, life, and motion. To be comforted, to be filled, to enter into possession of the whole wide earth, to behold God, nay to partake, as his own "sons," of his very nature, to have and to hold the Kingdom of Heaven itself—how different these satisfactions are from abiding in the shadow of the Almighty or dwelling in the secret place of the Most High or being made to lie down in pastures however green, or to wander by waters of quietness however

[26] Matt. 19:26. [27] Matt. 13:57; Mark 6:4; Luke 4:24; John 4:44.

unruffled. The peace and rest which the Psalmist pictures are beautiful in their negation of care and toil but the results which Jesus proposes throb with the intensity of the leadership of the "sons of God" in the kingdom of brotherhood throughout the world.

No one can read the ten commandments of Moses from Mt. Sinai along with Jesus' discourse from the new Sinai by the Sea of Galilee without feeling the magnificent prohibitory negatives of the decalogue pale before the radiant eight affirmatives of the beatitudes of Jesus. We are at once made aware that the souls of men are really capable of Godlikeness and that the earth is yet to be filled with the manifestation of their spiritual glory.

It is also interesting to note the affirmativeness with which Jesus treats what we call the main doctrines of theology. God, for him, is not the jealous God who punishes iniquity to the third and fourth generation. He is always a father who can, indeed, be severe with the unforgiving [28] but whose great prevailing quality is a beneficent love of surpassing power. Election is election to service.[29] Jesus chooses twelve in order to send them forth.[30] Salvation is not rescue from hell except subordinately and by implication. It is entering into or receiving eternal life.[31] The death of Christ is not to appease his Father's wrath but to infuse new life into the world. Failure to accept his death is to fail of having life.[32] He gave his life as a vicarious sac-

[28] Matt. 18:35.   [29] John 15:16.   [30] Matt. 10:5.
[31] John 3:16.   [32] John 6:51, 53, 54.

rifice not in the sense of a "rigid satisfaction, death for death," but as a ransom which bought for many that positive spiritual liberty which was so dear to his heart. Forgiveness is not merely letting an offense go unpunished. It is a total giving of the divine to the human. It is the Father's heart pouring itself into the heart of his child. It is the story of the Prodigal Son. It is the very essence of the gospel. Providence is an affirmative care for the individual man. Jesus makes his thought of it clear by changing the Old Testament negative phrase, "There shall not a hair of him fall to the earth," [33] to "The very hairs of your head are all numbered." [34] The Old Testament providence was one that protected its object from evil, allowing no hair to fall, but for Jesus the hairs are numbered with a view to their positive value and preservation. The change of wording is slight but by no means accidental.

This positiveness of Jesus' general attitude made him pick out the good in the people he met of whatever sort. He took them on their positive side. Economic questions might be involved in Mary's anointing. But certainly she meant it well. Therefore Jesus regarded her intent and glorified her deed. Goodness is goodness for him no matter how it takes effect or from whom it proceeds. He recognized the faith of the pagan centurion most heartily. He marveled gladly at the Syro-Phoenician woman's belief in him. He incorporated with his own work the irregular work of an outsider who was casting out demons. Electric light

---

[33] II Samuel 14:11; I Kings 1:52.   [34] Matt. 10:30; Luke 12:7.

and pure water are the same whether furnished by the authorized municipal plant or by private corporations. He had an affirmative toleration of and a positive delight in every form of goodness even when it failed to belong to regularly constituted authorities.

He loved the story of the Queen of Sheba because it depicted a character whose love of truth was so earnestly active that she traveled far to find an answer to her soul's questionings. It was part of Jesus' attitude of love toward all goodness anywhere.

Still more important is it to recognize that Jesus turned toward the goodness of the good rather than to the wickedness of the wicked. Jesus gives more than one summary of the law and the prophets. The Golden Rule, for example, compacts them all into itself.[35] So also does the great commandment of love.[36] But Jesus never sums up transgressions into one master sin. It has been left for the religious philosophers to discover the essence of sin. They may have succeeded completely but Jesus never made the attempt. His face was turned toward God and goodness. That was his attitude and its living fixity precluded any careful study in the unification of evil.

He has no parables of the kingdom of hell. Just as his beatitudes delighted in the heaven within the soul so his parables were parables of the Kingdom of God. He did, indeed, speak on one occasion of a hypothetical kingdom of Satan divided against itself,[37] but his adversaries furnished him the text and compelled the

---

[35] Matt. 7:12.　　[36] Matt. 22:37–40.　　[37] Matt. 12:26.

incidental utterance. He would never have used the illustration of his own motion and did not return to it. The exception, indeed, proves the rule, for it shows that the image was in men's minds and if Jesus had had a mind for the portrayal of the details of evil he could easily have matched the parables of the kingdom of God with a corresponding series of the kingdom of Satan. Nothing, indeed, but his bent toward holiness can account for the absence of such creations from his teachings. Nor has he any negative golden rule or portraiture of the principle of retaliation or reciprocity in evil. He indulged in no descriptions of Antichrist.

It is a great work to lift men out of barbarism, to remove from their lives the destructive exercise of the passions that degrade and destroy, to erect against evil a fence which prevents the incursions of the wild beast into society. This was no small part of the work of the Old Testament law. But Jesus takes men at just that point. He does not forbid his disciples to commit murder or bear false witness. He assumes that the wild gorges are closed up and the rugged mountains are leveled down. Then he says to those who are thus placed on the moral level of respectability, "Go forward in the life of self-devotion and active love." When the young ruler told him he had kept all the commandments, Jesus invited him to convert his effects into cash, apply the proceeds to the relief of the needy and join the itinerary of those who had taken up the cross as the mission of their lives. There was an average practice of politeness and mutual helpfulness in the society of his day but in presence of all this Jesus asked his disciples, "What do ye more than others?"

There was abundance of evil in Jesus' day needing rebuke. The Decalogue was sufficiently violated on every hand. Why did not Jesus spend more strength upon the enforcement of the prohibitions of evil? It must have been because he felt that the world needed a more affirmative religion, needed to practice the powers of active love and to enter with him upon such a campaign of goodness that it would have no time to be tempted by evil or any surplus energy to be spent in transgression. If it would only walk in the spirit it would not fulfil the lusts of the flesh.[38]

But, although Jesus assumed the Old Testament morality, he was obliged to take an attitude toward it, for the Old Testament scriptures were the Bible of his day. The attitude he took was what we should expect. He brought a new teaching. Did he then expect to put the old out of the way? Would he destroy the sacred laws and prophecies of Israel? No, he came not to destroy but to fulfil. There was an instinctive fear among Jewish leaders who listened to him that men inspired with his love to their fellows would not follow numbered commandments or arithmetically calculated traditions. Jesus meets this fear with his assertion. He would fulfil the whole law. Probably he meant to include the ceremonial as well as the moral codes, for both were detailed attempts to better the condition of mankind. Yet Jesus did destroy the outward form of these old laws as his enemies feared. He did it by filling

---

[38] Gal. 5:16.

them with a new and expansive life of love which was more than they could contain and which burst through them.

In no essential sense does the fledgling bird destroy the egg from which it comes. Only the shell is ruined. The egg itself is fulfilled, expanded and made wonderfully great. The butterfly does not destroy the caterpillar but only fulfils it. The dragon-fly by his inner force rends the veil of his old husk. The plates of sapphire mail come shining forth. He rests upon the limb of a tree. His short wings dry out and grow long. Then through the dewy crofts and pastures he darts like a living flash of light. So it is that the living love of Jesus fills the ancient husks of precepts so full that it bursts through them and leaves them behind.

This is the affirmative spirit of power, with which Jesus sought to fill every good but imperfect institution of his day. The law of ordinances contained in precepts was, indeed, abolished by Jesus. Christianity soon ceased to live within the Old Testament framework. But this result did not come because Jesus took a negative attitude toward the law, for he was made under the law and as far as possible conformed himself to it. Yet he viewed it positively and the very fulness of the life which he breathed into it destroyed the shell but gave birth to a new spirit.

CHAPTER VII

Attitude Toward the Mosaic Law

BUT the relation of Jesus to the Scripture of his day was of such a specially large and important character as to call for a further and fuller illustration and analysis. These we now attempt to give.

In spirit and temper the Old Testament of course represented a vast ethical and religious advance. This was true even of some of its precepts which to us have a very ferocious appearance, such as the *lex talionis* which demanded an eye for an eye and a tooth for a tooth. At a still earlier period the man who had lost an eye sought to take both eyes and even the very life of the man who had so injured him. He sought unlimited revenge. To confine the punishment to one eye was to make a sharp ethical advance. To take our own present-day standard of retribution or our Christian standard of forgiveness and judge an Old Testament custom or statute by it, is not only crude and unhistorical but also unjust. A code may be behind the standard we have attained, but if it is far ahead of what had previously obtained we should credit it with the spirit of positive advance. All advances of this kind are, as it were, advances *toward* an affirmative standpoint. They are a lessening of the distance between not doing wrong and the affirmativeness of love.

Isaiah's doctrine of a remnant of Israel that should return from captivity does not compare with Jesus' doctrine of the chosen few who were to spread his spirit and carry his kingdom into all the world. But Isaiah's doctrine is far more hopeful than that of Plato who not only tells us that the honest followers of wisdom are a very small remnant but advises them to keep still and mind their own business. Plato often advises men standing aside in the shelter of a wall in the midst of a storm of dust and hurricane of wind and enduring to behold the rest of men filled with iniquity if only they themselves may live their life clear of injustice and impiety and depart at last in peace.[1] Isaiah's task was tragic enough but he did not counsel his remnant to hide behind a wall. He sought to fill them with fire, with hope, with faith, even with joy and to make them believe in a future for themselves, for Israel, and even for the outside world.

It is also clear that the Old Testament here and there shows evidence of the Christian spirit before the Christian day. Joseph's forgiveness of his brethren, certain pearls of Christian thought which Job secreted in the deep sea of his agony, Isaiah's portrait of the Suffering Servant, Micah's formulation of the requirement of Jehovah are a few among numerous examples. It still remains true that Jesus introduced a new spirit and method and told the world a new secret. He directly

---

[1] Plato, *Republic VI*.

and firmly taught the insufficiency of the old law, which he quoted for that very purpose. He proposed a higher and better teaching, which, taking the old as a basis, should rise above it.

It must not be supposed that it was because his hearers lived up to the law of Moses that Jesus did not re-enact it. It may be true that Jesus carves what Moses has hewn, but the men of Jesus' day themselves had not even hewn to the lines which Moses gave them. A certain rich man whom Jesus reminded of the ethical table of the law declared that he was already keeping it. And Jesus looked upon him with a love which implied that his moral sincerity was exceptional. Jesus stood upon the high table-land of the Mosaic law and invited men's souls to a still higher career. But he was not talking to a nation that had themselves in practice reached those table-lands. He was not taking a people that were keeping themselves unspotted from the world and leading them forward along still loftier paths of active goodness. In dealing with a people that were just human beings he was taking up a different method from the Old Testament one. He came not to make men obey the laws of Moses or any other legislator, but to fill men with a new life which would legislate for itself.

The Decalogue said, "Thou shalt not kill." Jesus added that every man that was angry enough with his brother to kill him and would do so if wholly free from restraining circumstances stood in danger of the same judgment. Nay, further, a man must not even hold that resentful spirit which says to another, "You godless wretch," or "You son of a devil." Such a spirit and temper of soul lead to a terrible penalty. This may be said to make the law *spiritual* instead of external. That statement, however, falls far short of rising to the height of Jesus' great argument. It leaves the spiritual law still negative and sanctioned by the threat of penalty. The fact is that Jesus uses the old law in order to obtain a platform on which to advance. But once having taken his position with both feet on the floor of the soul he adds the positive step he had in mind from the outset. If you hate a man you must not simply be prepared for a reconciliation in case he comes your way, expresses regrets, makes advances, and proffers needed reparation.

You yourself must take the initiative. A sense of the state of things may come over you like a wave of pure air into the open window of a fetid room just as you are beginning an act of outward worship. It is very likely to come at that time. If it does, drop the thing you have in hand even if it be a valuable gift or costly sacrifice for the sanctuary. Let that whole matter go for the time being. Hunt up your man. Be reconciled. Then and not till then return to your worship. The paragraph must be read in its entirety. The injunction must be taken as a totality. The "Therefore" must involve the negative in the positive and carry it up to its culmination there.[2]

The old law, again, forbade practical perjury. A man must do as he had sworn. Promises made under

---

[2] Matt. 5:21–24.

oath must be lived up to fully and faithfully. But such a command tempts men to divide promises into two classes, those made under oath and those not so made. They may even get to thinking that while the first set must be sacredly kept, the second may be tampered with or broken. There were various degrees of promises and oaths in which one swore by heaven or by earth or by Jerusalem or by his head. These did not expressly include the name of God and hence had only a secondary sacredness. With all this casuistry Jesus pursues his usual affirmative method of inwardness and positiveness. An inwardly truthful and reverent soul would recognize the presence of God in everything. To swear by anything would be to swear by the God who was in it and owned it. Thus by recognizing God in every form of oath Jesus extends the territory of perfect sacredness into all of them. Then he takes one more step beyond all vicious verbal annexations by requiring within the soul that naked power of faithfulness which makes a man's unembroidered "yes" or "no" as good as his heaviest bond.[3]

In primitive times man threw his whole soul into his revenge. In the days of the law revenge was reduced to the exact measure of rigid justice. An eye for an eye and a tooth for a tooth. Jesus could not endure such cold negations. He completed the circuit by restoring the early warmth and heat of unlimited attack upon one's enemy. The injured man must gird on his weapons of love and faith and smite with his

---

[3] Matt. 5:33-37.

whole soul. His thought and intent must be: If a man by superior physical force robs me of one garment, I will watch my chance to insist on giving him another. If a soldier puts his burden upon my back and compels me, at the point of his pike, to carry it a mile and then contemptuously turns me off, I must be glad because he has further to go and with cheery face of my own accord trudge on with his pack for a second mile. These vivid maxims must be understood as principles. The follower of Jesus must no more think of dividing his conduct into destructive hate for his enemy and kindly conduct toward his friends than God would think of cutting off his sunlight along the line where the boundary fence divides the bad man's acres from the good man's or of leaving the first field dry while the second received the refreshing rain. The soul must be so full of love that it pours itself forth upon the evil and the good alike.[4]

Thus Jesus did away with the law by fulfilling it. What becomes of the law against murder for a man who is never under the dominion of anger but seeks loving commerce with all men, even the enemy and the injurer! What becomes of the law against adultery to the man who with perfect purity even of thought is seeking the higher life and the vision of the eternal? What becomes of the law against unfaithfulness to an oath for a man who has passed beyond the need of all oaths? What becomes of the law against excessive revenge to a man whose soul is one continuous outpour-

---

[4] Matt. 5:38-48.

ing of love toward all men and loves his enemies as well as he does his friends? This is the victory of the affirmative and empowered soul. This is the method and secret of Jesus.

Affirmativeness of love to men also rightly describes Jesus' use of the ceremonial law. This is the key to his practical treatment of it. It is hardly telling the whole truth to claim that Jesus practiced conformity to the ceremonial law. Sometimes he did and sometimes he did not, but the selective principle is not to be found in a classification of the ceremonies themselves so that he observed one class and disregarded another. He was governed simply by the dominance of his love for men. Leprosy made a man unclean ceremonially, and lepers were segregated.[5] But Jesus allowed these unclean persons to approach him and touched them.[6] Nevertheless he was likely to send lepers, whether singly or in company, to the priests for cleansing.[7]

There might also be conflicts among the laws themselves. The law requiring circumcision on the eighth day would conflict with the law of the Sabbath if the eighth day fell on the Sabbath. In that case the higher law superseded the lower. All good Jews agreed on this. In like manner Jesus insisted that the law of mercy should always prevail.[8]

It is interesting also to observe that Jesus sought in the Old Testament for principles that were positive, at least in form of statement, and thus were capable

---

[5] Lev. 13:45, 46. [6] Mark 1:41. [7] Mark 1:44; Luke 17:14.
[8] John 7:22–24.

of bearing a positive meaning. Jesus was asked on a certain occasion what was the great commandment in the law. He gave the now familiar reply that it was an all absorbing and powerful love to God and that it must be taken in connection with the other and similar commandment of love to one's neighbor.[9] The two commandments are separate matters in the Old Testament. It is significant that Jesus put them together. He did not desire to have the commandment in regard to our fellow men regarded as of subordinate and separate significance from the commandment of love to God. For love is not two but one and in his own soul Jesus never could for a moment think of them in any other way than as forming, when taken together, a kind of golden rule and summary of the whole work and worship of man.

Let us bear in mind, however, that the Old Testament idea of love to God must be interpreted in terms of the Old Testament law. Love was the fulfilling of the law. Many of the commandments which the Old Testament love could fulfill were negative. A man must love God by not having any other God, by not making any image of any God, by not taking God's name in vain, by not working on the Sabbath. The love of God then, however lofty, was in the eyes of the law largely expressed in negatives.

The case was the same with love to one's neighbor.[10] It was framed in a context of prohibitions. No one can read the Old Testament chapter without feeling

---

[9] Mark 12:28–34; Matt. 22:34–40.   [10] Lev. 19:18.

that the frame controls the motto in its center. It is the old story: Thou shalt love they neighbor by not reaping the corners of thy field, by not robbing him, by not keeping back his wages, by not cursing him for his defective hearing or tripping him up for sport because he is blind, by not being influenced in matters of judgment by the wealth or station of a man, by not being a tale-bearer and by not hating or bearing a grudge.

There is also a species of universalism and even missionary spirit in the Old Testament. In Abraham all the nations of the earth were to be blessed and the ends of the earth were to see the salvation of the Lord. But the ancient Jew did not love outside peoples as outsiders. He loved them proleptically. He kept the actual outpouring of affection in reserve against the time when they should adopt the religion of his own nation and bring tribute to it. But Jesus forbids any such moratorium of affection. The love which Jesus intends must also be interpreted in the terms of his commandments and these are affirmative. They include giving the cloak, going the second mile, blessing one's enemies, lending without hope of return and, as his whole teaching shows, doing active, inventive, and initiative good of all sorts under all circumstances to all men.

The term "neighbor" has quite different connotations in the two Testaments. In the Old it means "the children of thy people." [11] With Jesus it includes Sa-

---

[11] Lev. 19:18.

maritans and those that despitefully use us. The old law told men to pitch the camp of love in Israel, to intrench and fortify it thoroughly and set guards everywhere to see that the commandments of love was observed inside the entire pale. But Jesus sent men out on aggressive campaigns to bless the enemy beyond the entrenchments, including even the far-away persecutor and the evil-disposed. There must be both a positive outflow in the love and an extension in the territory of its operation. The Mosaic command of love was affirmative in form and it spoke of an affection of the soul. As a verbal framework it met Jesus' two demands of inwardness and of affirmativeness. He had the leisure of time enough in which to fill it with a meaning that would make it expressive of his own essential mission. Many other instances of Jesus' selection of affirmative texts from the Old Testament will be given later, but this one is sufficient to show his peculiar desire to find in the authorized scriptures of his people forms of statement which combine inwardness with affirmativeness.

It is also worthy of note that Jesus did not cite the negative commands of the old law in order to say that being negative they were not needed. He did not tell men to pay no attention to prohibitions of evil. He would not take a negative attitude toward even a negative command. On the contrary he affirmed it more strongly provided the command was ethically right, and gave it his sanction even while he implied its insufficiency. This might be partially due to a wise practical regard for the sacred scriptures of his people which he himself certainly regarded as inspired. But his unhesitating criticism of those scriptures shows the liberty with which he handled them. His affirmative regard for the good negatives in the Bible of his people must, I think, be attributed to the absolute affirmativeness of his soul toward all genuine expressions of goodness of whatever form. He did not treat the good as an enemy of the best but as a stepping stone toward it.

It was like the relief which comes at last in learning one of the arts. Rule after negative rule is cautiously and earnestly obeyed at first. The negative rules at last are summarized by being blended into a general instinctive avoidance. Portion after portion of constructive performance is meanwhile achieved until at last the one great principle rules and controls at every step. Detailed rules are observed as certainly as ever but unconsciously. The art is just as complex and elaborate as ever but the complexity and elaborateness are attended to with such ease that the exertion is quite unrealized. The musician sweeps through his symphony feeling nothing but its theme.

The positive treatment which Jesus gave to the law he also extended to many passages outside the Books of Moses. Into them Jesus infused the transforming power of his spiritual positiveness. Isaiah, for example, has much to say about women but it is of denunciation all compact. Nothing is spared. The affected nicety of their walk, the lavish variety of their dress, their display of jewelry, their headgear and their perfumery, their entire luxury and wantonness are itemized in the

catalogue of his scorn.[12] Yet all this castigation is negative. Its absence from the words of Jesus is conspicuous. Luke is the gospel for women, but in his narra-
tive the sinner at Simon's house receives no scourging
from Jesus' lips.[13] It is not the sins but the services of
women that are recited.[14] The other evangelists less
fully but not less clearly than Luke write to the same
effect. There is not a harlot from whom Jesus draws
away his tunic, and not a few of them enter his kingdom with penitence and sacrificial ministeries. The
contrast is extraordinary and characteristic. The stern
and pitiless prophetic rebuke of the harlot gives place
in Jesus to free acceptance and even eloquent cham-
pionship, because she herself is no longer at heart a
harlot. The passion of her life which negated all her
goodness has been changed into a white and penitent
passion of positive purity and grateful service.

Another example is the figure of the marriage of a
god to his people. Its use in Hebrew literature is large.
Israel's maker is her husband and the relationship is
elaborated with wonderful tenderness and force.[15]
Hosea makes effective use of the allegory. Jesus adopts
the figure in his own way. He condenses the whole Old
Testament negative element of unfaithfulness into a
single passing adjective. He lives in an adulterous generation.[16] The main strength of his use of the figure
goes entirely to the overflowing joy of a wedding
festival. He is the bridegroom and his "best men" share

---

[12] E.g., Isa. 3:16–24.   [13] Luke 7:36–50.
[14] Luke 8:2 f; 23:55 f; 24:1 f. et al.
[15] Isa. 49:14–22; 50:1; 51:17–20; 52:1 f; 54:1.   [16] Matt. 12:39.

his joy. His new marriage to the souls of men is a thing that overflows with affirmative joy. Such being its character, the negative feature of fasting is necessarily excluded. Fasting has no place at a wedding and a wedding is Jesus' chosen emblem for his own life and work.[17]

There is a good instance of Jesus' large and positive handling of Old Testament ideas in his appropriation of the phrase "son of man." It was a very comprehensive term, ranging all the way from the insignificance of the poorest and commonest human being [18] to the heavenly enthronement and everlasting dominion of the mystic representative man of Daniel's vision.[19] The range of the phrase corresponded to the development of Jesus' career. Therefore he laid his hand upon it and fulfilled it from his humblest declaration that he had not where to lay his head,[20] to the suggestion of power which he made at last before the high priest.[21] No one acquainted with the times in which Jesus lived can trace his uses of the title without feeling anew the combination of practical wisdom and affirmative effect with which he employed it. Originally a negative term of humility, Jesus filled it as applied to himself with a more and more positive content.

So also with the prophetic and Judaistic idea of the Kingdom of God. Jewish legalism even in the most earnest and spiritual hands did much toward burying the idealism of the Kingdom of God which lived in

---

[17] Mark 2:18 f.   [18] Psalm 8:4.   [19] Daniel 7:13 f.
[20] Luke 9:58.   [21] Matt. 26:64.

the pages of the great prophets. Yet legalism by no means completely obscured the old conception. Jesus with his spiritual idealism treated the conception practically and affirmatively. He did not give it a name. It already had that. But he did give it a local habitation. He did indeed call his followers a little flock and he taught them that they had a spiritual father in heaven but he also said, "Fear not, little flock; it is your Father's good pleasure to give you the Kingdom." In a very practical sense Jesus founded the Kingdom of God in Galilee by bringing it down from heaven to earth, bringing it from the future to a place near at hand. There is a peculiarly positive tone and ring in Jesus' first words in the Gospel of Mark, "The Kingdom of God is at hand." [22]

The positive method of Jesus changes morality to religion. Morality is apt to be conceived of as negative. The inscription over the Old Testament morality was "Thou shalt not." This negative morality, however, was touched with emotion and idealism in law and psalm and prophecy. It was often connected with Israel's God in a spirit of passionate devotion. But in Jesus' day under the Scribal and Temple regime the emotion had been largely eliminated. Religion included a series of minute ceremonial observances. God had been retired behind priests and farther away yet behind hierarchies of angels. The act of obedience had little relation, if any, to him. Not that there was no religion in men's hearts, not that they did not sometimes

[22] Mark 1:15.

send out the warm cry of thanksgiving or the wild cry for deliverance. But the catalogued and codified acts were done as a kind of ethical observance somewhat apart from the relation of the heart to God.

By unifying all of men's ethical acts under one principle of love and by making that love an outwelling fountain whose water was one of quality, whether it flowed toward God or toward man, Jesus made morality into religion and religion into morality. The helpful word a man spoke was the direct outcome of the life of God within him and therefore was religious. The life of God within him was a warm ethical unity and therefore its issue was an ethical thing. Acts done in the Old Testament day in obedience to the law of Moses, being items in a code, could be considered one after another as separate acts or even as embodiments of principle without special relation to Jehovah. But no one can point to any part of the pure continuous flame of Jesus' life and say, "This was ethical not religious." For in him the multitudinous items of ethics had been fused into one self-legislating flame and the flame was love.

Another effect of Jesus' positive handling of the Old Testament lay in changing the letter into the Spirit. Like a blind man spelling out raised characters, the people of Jesus' day felt the precepts of the law one at a time, occasionally putting them together into principles and sub-principles as the blind man makes out his words and sentences. But Jesus, as it were, opened the eyes of the blind. They no longer saw words or even sentences as such. They saw the ideas they stood for. They took in the whole paragraph at a glance. The words and letters were all there but the meaning or the spirit was the thing which was grasped. If the page were taken away the man could rewrite it for substance out of his own soul. The law of the spirit of life is Christ. Jesus made men free from the written letter and its precisions of meaning. In so far as "the letter" was right they grasped its spirit, and wherever it was not right the spirit within them was able to rewrite it in proper form.

By this positive method Jesus became the creator of a new religion. If the maxims of the Sermon on the Mount are taken as mere maxims, Jesus becomes a rival of Moses. For he gives a collection of precepts and ordinances. But if these sayings of his are principles in the form of maxims, the principles are merely different sides or aspects of the one principle of positive love. They are correlated to one another like electricity, magnetism, light, and motion, as different forms of that one force. If electricity is new, then Jesus brought a new religion to his people.

As the Old Testament precepts could be summed up in the commandment of love more negatively understood, so the New Testament precepts of Jesus can be summed up in the commandment of love more positively and affirmatively understood. With Jesus the principle of positive love differentiated itself into every form of good precept. The Old Testament commandment of love was a condensed summary of prevailing negative commandments. The New Testament principle of love was the indwelling spirit of the

Heavenly Father. A legal summary reaches the soul from outside and is not creative. A positively creative summary must be the life of love within the soul, a life which creates and legislates for itself and makes an infinite number of different laws for itself as it goes along.

CHAPTER VIII

Scripture Passages He Most Loved

THERE is one very striking exception to the statements made concerning Jesus' relation to the Mosaic law. Of his own accord and without any suggestion of it in the Pharisaic attack, Jesus does for once cite a single commandment from the Decalogue not for the purpose of revising or enlarging it but just as it stands in its Old Testament form. The Pharisees accused him of transgressing the tradition of the elders. He replied by accusing them of transgressing the commandments of God. The commandment he cites is the fifth—"Honor thy father and thy mother." It is the only affirmative member of the Decalogue. In a world of moral negatives which insisted upon prohibitions and multiplied them endlessly, Jesus turned to the one affirmative that stood out sharply among the negatives.

May there not be as much significance in this fact as there is in Paul's reference to the tenth commandment? In explaining his religious experience Paul tells us he should not have realized the power of sin if the law had not said "Thou shalt not covet." He was exceedingly zealous for the law and examined himself upon it in the light of conscience. The majestic voice spoke to him and said, "Thou shalt have no other Gods"; and with a clear conscience bearing him witness he answered, "I have none." "Thou shalt not make unto thee any graven image." "I do not." "Thou shalt not kill." "There, too, I am guiltless." "Thou shalt not commit adultery." "I never have committed it." But, "Thou shalt not covet." "Covet? Covet? Why, why—that is a thing of the soul. It is inward. I do not do the forbidden things, but to possess an inward state of not wanting to do them at all—who can be guiltless there? If that is what God requires, I am undone. God have mercy upon me!" So law "slew" him and brought him to Christ. But it was the tenth shaft, not any one of the other nine that went home to his soul. He would not have felt what sin was but for the law, and for one particular law at that, "Thou shalt not covet." [1] The one commandment to which Jesus gives a similar isolation is no less significant, though in a different way. The tenth commandment was the only one that went inward. The fifth is the only one of the ten that calls for affirmative conduct. As the tenth commandment reveals the form of Paul's experience of consecration, so in a sense the fifth may suggest to us the form of Jesus' religion. That form was positive, life-expressing, life-giving and life-demanding service.

Jesus shows marked preference for the affirmative,

---

[1] Romans 7:7. See the fuller discussion in B. W. Robinson, *Life of Paul*, Chap. III.

the overflowing, the dynamic. The three books of the Bible which had his special regard seem to be the latter part of Isaiah, the Book of Jonah, and Daniel.

Matthew finds in Isaiah the prediction of the birth of Jesus,[2] the description of the work of John the Baptist,[3] the glad outburst of gospel light in Galilee,[4] and the practical spirit in which Jesus conducted his ministry.[5] It is in the same prophet that he finds the hardening of the Jewish heart against Jesus predicted.[6] The triumphal entry is also found foretold by him.[7] It is the language of the same prophet that is so frequently utilized throughout the New Testament to describe the sufferings of Jesus as the lamb of God that takes away the sin of the world.[8] These references are made by the evangelists themselves and are as various in character as the events which fulfill them.

Jesus himself, however, according to these same evangelists makes references to the same prophet. His references, unlike theirs, have a certain characteristic in common. They are the manifestations of a forthgoing, campaigning, self-revealing, self-announcing, self-proclaiming spirit. The evangelists themselves use Isaiah the "evangelical prophet" so predominantly because looking backward at Jesus' finished career the sayings of the prophet seem to them to fit the master's career so well. Jesus' own citations were made because he turned to Isaiah, especially the later portion of

---

[2] Matt. 1:23; Isa. 7:14.   [3] Matt. 3:3; Isa. 40:3.
[4] Matt. 4:15, 16; Isa. 9:1, 2.   [5] Matt. 12:18–21; Isa. 42:1 ff.
[6] Matt. 13:14 f; Isa. 6:9, 10.   [7] Matt. 21:5; Isa. 62:11.
[8] John 1:29, 36; Isa. 53:7; Acts 8:32.

Isaiah, as having a spirit kindred to his own. Isaiah gives us the very word for "evangelism" or the "gospel." It rings with the "good news" of return, redemption, illumination, universal righteousness and world-wide salvation. It is the positiveness of the book that constituted its attractiveness for Jesus. Hence he took his stand upon it at the very outset in announcing himself in the synagogue at Nazareth. He found the place in the book which identified the working of the spirit of the Lord with proclaiming good news and with a life overflowing with universal blessings.[9]

A fragmentary reading may create an impression of denunciatory or negative use of Isaiah by Jesus on the occasion of his cleansing the temple. That act is almost universally characterized as a negative "cleansing," a casting-out of evil practices. It is even hinted that Jesus was carried away by his passion against sacrilege. We have seen that this is not a true account of the matter. It is the court of the Gentiles which Jesus cleanses with the positive purpose of restoring it as "a house of prayer for all the nations." [10] Putting an end to sacrilege was merely a subordinate and preliminary necessity. The essence of the act is not the sudden ejection but the permanent and proper use of the temple. The main issue is not between sanctity and sacrilege. This is why the quotation does not stop with "house of prayer" but adds "for all the nations." It was characteristic of him to refer to Scripture in a large and comprehensive way. He had the context of

---

[9] Luke 4:18 f; Isa. 61:1 f.   [10] Isa. 56:7; Mark 11:17.

his passage in mind, or rather the total spirit of the section. That spirit is abundantly evident to any reader. It is a spirit of joyful occupation of God's house of prayer by all peoples, not only the gathered outcasts of Israel but the innumerable outsiders that are also gathered there with them.[11]

Another book that Jesus loved was Jonah. Brief as the book is, the gospels not only connect it with the resurrection but with the Jewish demand for a sign and with the judgment.[12] The reference to Jonah's being three days and three nights in the belly of the whale [13] does not occur in Mark or Luke, while the reference to the preaching of Jonah is found, and found a second time, in Matthew,[14] and is used and repeated in Luke.[15] It would seem as if Jesus specially favored the reference to the book as a whole. He certainly regarded his work with his generation as in some sort parallel to, though greater than, Jonah's work with his. "They repented at the preaching of Jonah, but more than Jonah is here." [16] The commission of Jonah was to an outside city which was the traditional and inveterate enemy of his own people.[17] It was just such a God of overflowing and far-traveling missionary love that Jesus recognized in his own heavenly Father. This affirmative affection of God for all men including children and cattle [18] accounts for the indications in the gospels of Jesus' love for the book in question.

---

[11] Isa. 56:6–8.   [12] Matt. 12:39–41.   [13] Matt. 12:40.
[14] Matt. 16:4.   [15] Luke 11:32.   [16] Luke 11:29, 30, 32.
[17] Jonah 4:2.   [18] Jonah 4:11.

There is one other book to which Jesus evidently turned with favor. He cites it concisely, but we must bear in mind that compacting as much meaning as possible into the briefest verbal compass was a principle with Jesus. In accordance with this principle he had a way of citing a single phrase or clause which carried with it a large fringe of suggestion. The Book of Daniel was full of the general idea of a Kingdom of God and of the rule of a symbolic Son of Man as distinguished from the rule of symbolic beasts. There is scarcely need to remark that these ideas were especially prominent with Jesus. There was great practical value in the fact that the terms used by Daniel such as "Son of Man" and "Kingdom of God" were somewhat vague and mystic in their meaning. They were almost indefinitely expansible and might be filled with as wide a range of meanings as the range of Jesus' life and teachings suggested.

There was also a positively growing and conquering spiritual power running through all the book which no less than its practical usability endeared it to Jesus. It was akin to his own consciousness of affirmative, inward and spiritual power going forth and taking practical and growing effect in the hearts of men and in the external world. It is in this light that we are to understand his reference to the falling stone which should "scatter as dust" those on whom it fell.[19] It was the spiritual stone cut out of the mountain without hands which was to pulverize all material oppositions,

---

[19] Luke 20:18.

so that natural elemental forces like the wind would scatter them. The stone itself would fill the earth with its single mountainous mass.[20] Jesus himself lived too close to the modesty of nature to use such imagery as Daniel's in making his parables of the Kingdom of God. But the mystic universalism of the book and the sense of progressive power furnish him with some of his most effective recurring phrases as well as with allusions suggestive of positive power. It was not the destructiveness of scattering as dust which Jesus liked but the stupendous growth and the architectural, constructive use as a "corner stone." [21]

In addition to these books to which Jesus especially turned as a whole there are scattered throughout the Old Testament individual passages and symbols to which he turned for a similar reason. The lifting up of the brazen serpent was an act of positive healing and life-saving.[22] The pillar of fire was a living and moving light.[23] The water rushing from the smitten rock of the wilderness, like every other spring of water, was to the poetic Hebrew conception a thing that was literally alive.[24] David's eating the shewbread when fleeing from Saul [25] represented a large and royal overriding of ceremonial sanctity by human need. The priestly kneading and mixing of meal offerings with oil [26] represented the overruling power of the large general requirements for worship.[27]

Very striking, too, is the Scripture to which Jesus

[20] Daniel 2:34, 35, 44, 45.   [21] Matt. 21:42–44.   [22] John 3:14.
[23] John 8:12.   [24] John 7:37.   [25] I Sam. 21:6.
[26] Num. 28:9, 10.   [27] Matt. 12:3–5.

turned for a characterization of John the Baptist. The forerunner himself looked upon his work as negative and preparatory. In the true spirit of the Old Testament law he called upon men to cease from extortion, violence and every form of transgression. But Jesus named John Elijah because, as with Elijah, the keynote of his life was force—the force of righteousness. But still more specifically in speaking of John's work Jesus connects it with a particular passage in Malachi where the prophet represents Elijah as doing a beautiful affirmative work in turning the hearts of the fathers to the children and the hearts of the children to their fathers [28]—not a negative work at all but a unifying and constructive one, a work to whose large lines Jesus gives the aspect of "restoring all things." [29]

God's holiness throughout the Old Testament retains a negative flavor. But Jesus associated it with the active offices of the Holy Spirit and gave it a positive meaning. In the Old Testament the word "holy" is generally used to point out God's withdrawal from some presumptuous intrusion of man on his majesty or to rebuke men's unworthy thoughts of him. For Jesus God's spirit is a driving power, an energy of service.

Jesus gave many negative texts an affirmative turn. There were not enough affirmative texts which he could directly cite or cite effectively for a present purpose. His free and powerful spirit, moreover, was always ready to turn any expression of the earlier covenant, whatever its context might be, for the pur-

---

[28] Mal. 4:5 f.   [29] Mark 9:12.

pose of pointing his own moral, or intensifying his own tuition. This readiness was thoroughgoing, and numerous instances of it have incidentally come before us already. With Jesus "salt" was not antiseptic but gave savor and flavor. The hairs of men's heads were not watched as they fell but numbered to keep them from falling. The brazen serpent saved the lives of those who looked at it but those who looked at Jesus not only did not perish but had eternal life. Loving one's neighbor as one's self is not only not doing prohibited things to him but discovering and doing all possible things that make for his welfare. In thus transforming a negative or neutral passage into a positive one Jesus often did not hesitate to give it a deeper meaning than the Old Testament writer intended it to convey. The gloom or glow in which he saw a Scripture passage was not infrequently a hue of his own insight fresh borrowed from his heart.

In this same spirit also Jesus alters Isaiah's parable of the vineyard from a story of failure and destruction to a story of transferred superintendence and fruitage. In Isaiah the evil of the vineyard is its bad fruit. It brings forth wild grapes. In Isaiah the wall of the vineyard is broken down and the land given up to the tramp of passing feet and to rainlessness and thorns. The vineyard has no future. Jesus turns these destructive negations into hopeful positives. Everything is done with reference to fruit, and ultimate success results. The wicked farmers are evicted, new tenants are put in, the fruit is rendered in season to the rightful owner and all goes well.[30]

---

[30] Isa. 5:1–7; Matt. 21:33–43.

One more illustration may be added because it shows how he could take the most destructive results of corruption as pictured by an old-time prophet and turn them into evidences of the spiritual intensity which his gospel required. The prophet Micah, in giving a description of his nation's moral corruption, inserts telling details of their untrustworthiness. Men should beware of having any confidences with their neighbors or friends. They should keep their mouths shut even to their wives. A man's own son dishonored his father. The daughter rose up against her mother and the daughter-in-law against her mother-in-law. A man's enemies were those of his own house.[31]

Jesus utilizes the passage in giving his commission to his disciples and repeats the prophet's details. He gives his followers a beautiful and gladsome but pure and holy commission. They will need to be fearless heralds. They must confess him amid whatever dangers. His message which they give will set a man against his father and a daughter against her mother and will in short entail the very divisions which Micah enumerates. Nor will Jesus permit the idea that the forceful characters in these divisions are those that do the persecuting. The positive force is to reside rather in the persecuted. The son is set against the father not because the father accepts Christ and the son therefore uses him despitefully. It is the son who confesses Christ with such inward intensity that it sets him in necessary opposition to his unbelieving father.[32]

---

[31] Micah 7:5, 6.   [32] Matt. 10:16-39.

The forces of hate and corruption in the Old Testament world and in the world of Jesus' day were so intense that they furnished a better illustration of personal earnestness for the gospel than the activities of men who were good. Jesus wishes to enforce intensity of spirit. It is remarkable that he does not hesitate for this purpose to take the negative intensity of corrupt and destructive passion in the Micah quotation, and by giving it a positive turn make it illustrate the intensity and initiative of spiritual courage which his gospel requires. His powerful soul laid hold of intensity and initiative wherever he saw them at their climax.

Thus Jesus used the Mosaic law and the other Scriptures of his day with freedom. The freedom, however, was governed by a single unifying principle. The fountainful and dynamic force of his own spirit appropriated whatever similarly forceful utterances the Old Testament contained, whether affirmative or negative in form and whatever their meaning in their own context. If the form was a positive statement, he adopted it. If the positive form was used to cover a range of negative goodness, he did not on that account hesitate to utilize it and add his own details of affirmative goodness to the items it embraced. If, on the other hand, the positiveness was directly evil he utilized its intensity and ignored the evil. To the negative correctness of conduct which the Old Testament enjoined he added a passionate enthusiasm of consecration to a life of love whose active force of its own accord made every necessary sacrifice. In a word, the overflowing, affirmative, and dynamic power of his own purely positive spirituality appropriated from the Scriptures everything which even partially reflected this supreme quality of his being. He revised or enlarged into harmony with it everything which fell short of its ideal passion of forthgoing, beneficent love.

PART IV

THE POSITIVE TEACHING

CHAPTER IX

The Nature of the Human Soul

THE special quality of fundamental positive action
which inhered in Jesus' idea of God and the human
soul may be illustrated from Goethe's *Faust*. That
majestic passage plunges back into eternity and takes
a position prior to creation. It mentions the Word and
then goes on to assign to this Word, as the expression of God's thought, a living, outgoing and creative
quality such as it has in the fifty-fifth of Isaiah. When
Goethe's Faust discusses the passage in John he points
the contrast we have in mind:

> 'Tis written: "In the Beginning was the Word."
> Here am I balked: who, now, can help afford?
> The *Word?*—impossible so high to rate it;
> And otherwise must I translate it,
> If by the Spirit I am truly taught,
> Then thus: "In the Beginning was the *Thought*."
> This first line let me weigh completely,
> Lest my impatient pen proceed too fleetly.
> Is it the *Thought* which works, creates, indeed?
> "In the Beginning was the *Power*," I read.
> Yet, as I write, a warning is suggested,
> That I the sense may not have fairly tested.

> The Spirit aids me: now I see the light!
> "In the Beginning was the *Act*," I write.[1]

The primal thing is full of action and expression. This creative power has not to do with the unacting calm of Nirvana, not with God in repose but with God in expression and action. Doubtless the ever-tranquil God was there "in the beginning," but just because the Gospel in its profoundest depth is essentially a thing of expression, action, and affirmation, when Faust finishes by saying, "In the beginning was the *Act*," his poetry happens to be not altogether out of accord, so far as words go, with the thought of Jesus.

Jesus did, indeed, teach that God is a Father. Little by little as we read use after use which he makes of the conception we come at last to see that it connotes his sovereign and total view of God's inmost character. It has dominant significance in his teaching. But it is the positive life and present power with which he makes the Father a living Father who has sent him and is with him and is ready to play the part for every man, that particularly marks his doctrine of the Fatherhood of God. When we speak of the "doctrine" of the Fatherhood of God we are often in danger of going astray, just as when we speak of God's omnipresence we are in danger of failing to practice the presence of God. What Jesus insists on is not the Fatherhood of God in general but the effective, fountainful, outpouring Father himself.

It would not be hard to give in terms of "Father" and "Son" an outline sketch of Hebrew history from

---

[1] Goethe, *Faust*, Part I, iii. Tr. by Bayard Taylor.

the Egyptian bondage to the return of the exiles: Thou shalt say unto Pharaoh, Thus saith the Lord, Israel is my Son, Even my first-born. When Israel was a child I loved him and called my son out of Egypt. I taught Ephraim also to walk, taking them by their arms. And in the wilderness thou hast seen that the Lord thy God bare thee as a man doth bear his son, all the way that ye went, until ye came into this place. I have nourished and brought up children and they have rebelled against me. Thou shalt also consider in thine heart, that, as a man chasteneth his son, so the Lord thy God chasteneth thee. Thou art our Father, though Abraham knoweth us not and Israel doth not acknowledge us; thou, O Lord, art our father, our redeemer, from everlasting is thy name. Is Ephraim my dear son? Is he a pleasant child? For since I spake against him I do earnestly remember him still: therefore my bowels are troubled for him; I will have mercy upon him, saith the Lord. I will cause them to walk by the rivers of waters in a straight way, wherein they shall not stumble. For I am a father to Israel and Ephraim is my first-born. The children of Judah and the children of Israel shall be gathered together, and they shall be put among the children and shall be given a pleasant land and a goodly heritage and they shall call me, My Father, and shall not turn away from me.

Jesus gives the conception a tender, concrete, factual power by seeing a father's hand sprinkle the rain, send abroad the morning sunshine, dress up the field flowers in their coats of many colors, and feed the chirping birds, while his heart saddens when one of them falls out of a tree. It is the peculiarly positive power which throbs through Jesus' expressions that makes his "Father" a new revelation and differentiates his view of God from the Old Testament view. The mosaic we made out of the Old Testament parental passages is a mosaic only. It could not have been made of any one author. For the staple material shows God as King. With the whole literature under one's eye, "Father" is as secondary a word in the Old Testament as "King" is with Jesus. The former says, "He who sometimes speaks with you as a father is your eternal King." The latter says, "He who for centuries has called himself your king is now finally unveiled as your eternal Father." The ancient family of Israel was a kingdom whose monarch was God. But Jesus' new kingdom is a family whose God is their heavenly Father. It is only a transfer of emphasis. But the transfer marks a revelation. And the revelation is in the emphasis.

Jesus brought out the truth of God's fatherhood as one brings a jewel cut with many facets out of the darkness, where it was a strain upon the eyes to see it or make out its shape, into the sunlight, where, as he turns it about before men's eyes, some new light is ever flashing forth from some new facet. The forthgoing quality of the Father's love is remarkably evident in the parable of the Lost Sheep. Montefiore, the Jewish commentator, remarks regarding the parable of the Lost Sheep, that this idea of God as actively searching does not occur anywhere in Jewish literature.[2]

Fatherhood, in other words, is an affirmative idea, a

---

[2] B. W. Robinson, *Sayings of Jesus*, Chap. XIV.

constructive power with Jesus. It is so vigorous that it builds the brotherhood of man. Man's greatest danger is that he will not receive this power of God's Fatherhood and become so intensely his son that he will perforce treat all men as his brothers.[3] It is thus that Jesus feels himself to be God's own Son and, judging others by himself, thinks that the power of God's Fatherhood, as he feels it and enforces it, can be extended to them.

There is a way of saying, "Come and confess your sin and be forgiven and be at peace with God." That was not exactly the way of Jesus. He made God's Fatherly love so overflowing that he could say, "If you will go to him just as you are, you will receive all the blessings that come to a Son. Let no sense of lost sonship make you seek the position of a hired servant, for God will be infinitely glad to reinstate you to the very full." The essential element in God's Fatherhood, then, is its affirmative abundance toward men. The Father sees the son afar off, is moved with compassion, runs, falls on his neck, kisses him. He brings out the best clothes for the returning son, puts the best possible luxuries upon the table, and suspends all work in order to have a joyous outburst of music and dancing.

Jesus' view of God helps to understand his view of the human soul. He saw the soul as an essentially active, radiating, outpouring thing. The Old Testament details of duty were negative in comparison.

[3] Matt. 6:14 f; 18:21 f, 35.

Jesus made that negative spirit of devotion into an active and affirmative passion. The passion was to go forth into the ways of life legislating for itself as it went along. Jesus was himself a fountain of love. Hence he viewed other men as capable of a similar outpouring. His view of the soul as active appears as the only natural view for him. His sympathy identified him with other men to such an extent that he judged them by himself. He taught men that they must somehow gather up and fuse all itemized and listed duties in a single glowing spirit of love which sent forth a single outpouring stream. He certainly had an eye for the historical development of this conception. The passages he cited from the Old Testament and his treatment of them show as much. But he did not seek to put men through any such process. Where preliminary steps were necessary he insisted that they be taken at once and put out of the way as a part of the plunge into the new life.

Other conceptions were current in Jesus' day; there was the conception of man as receptive and wrought upon by outside matters. The disciples sometimes ate food without previously washing their hands. Scrupulous Jews would not eat without washing them carefully according to directions. If they had been out to the market-place they even took a bath before eating. Otherwise some particle of uncleanness might be taken into their mouths along with the food. Outside circumstances made men clean or unclean. But Jesus said, "It is not that which goes into a man that defiles him. It is that which comes out of him." That which goes in at the mouth nature takes care of by cleansing and eliminating processes of her own. The entire figure or parable strikingly illustrates Jesus' fundamental view of the soul as active.

There are many things that do enter into the man and do defile him. Into the mouth itself, in the material form of excessive strong drink, does enter the cursed habit that sets the whole man on fire of hell. It is at the mouth that the liquid enemy enters that steals away the brain. It is at the mouth that excessive and Epicurean food enters and produces fatty degeneration of the soul. Drunkenness and gluttony, sins in the use of the things that enter the mouth, do defile men with the filth of the gutter, defile them body and soul. If we include the other senses, the case becomes worse yet. Into the soul through the unguarded gate of hearing come the foul images that do in fact reach the heart and terribly defile and destroy it. How easily Jesus might have turned from the mint and anise of eating with unwashen hands to the weightier matters of gluttony, drunkenness and the evil use of the receptive sense organs in general. But he conceives of the soul as acting and pouring forth. It is not a reservoir but a fountain, not a thing that absorbs but a thing that produces. This is the conception which he is determined to have everybody get, the multitudes as well as the disciples. He assembles them around himself again for this special purpose and imperatively insists upon their listening to it closely and understanding it clearly.[4]

It was with similar intent that Jesus turned the

---

[4] Matt. 15:10-20.

Pharisaic cleansings of cups and platters into a figure all his own. Some of the Pharisees made the outside surfaces of their life-cups clean while the inside, the heart, was full of extortion and excess. But Jesus' use of the figure involves much more than a contrast between the outside and the inside of a Pharisee's life. Matthew's report clearly reflects Jesus' vision of the soul as an active thing. The cup spills over constantly. It is in vain to wipe off soilure from its outside. If the inside is full of badness it is sure to go over the brim and foul the outside. Make the inside clean by filling it with what is clean. Then the outside too will become clean. The very overflow will make it so. When Jesus had the soul in mind he could not think of a cup or platter whose contents did not spill over onto the outside. They were too active for that. "Cleanse first the inside of the cup and of the platter that the outside thereof may become clean also." [5]

It is in the light of this ideal and fundamental conception of the soul as positive and actively affirmative that we best understand Jesus' two complementary assertions that he that was not for him was against him. Neutrality was impossible just because the soul was essentially active either for good or for evil. It was for the same reason also that his disciples could not serve God and Mammon howsoever successful some may seem to be in that duplex undertaking.

The impossibility of the soul's inactivity is indicated in a large number of passages. A tree bears fruit. But

---

[5] Matt. 23:25, 26.

does a good tree bear bad fruit or a bad tree bear good fruit? The mouth is an active orifice because the active abundance of the heart is back of it. Even idle words, like the flippant charge of collusion with Beelzebub, however smoothly uttered, would be brought up for account in the day of judgment because the mouth that spoke also had behind it an actively evil heart.[6]

Jesus' story of the empty soul is vivid and picturesque. The bad spirit leaves the house of the soul, wanders through waterless places and returns for a fuller and more absolute occupancy. But the emptiness of the house was the most portentous feature. There had been one bad tenant. There would be eight. Between the two occupancies was a vacancy. But it was an inviting vacancy. The very cleanness and the new decorations made the apartment attractive. Jesus may have referred to the ceremonial and decorative cleanness of some Pharisaic hearts from which the demon of gross transgression had been expelled and to which in company with others the demon was to return and thus make the condition of the soul really worse than ever.[7] Or he may have referred to the temporarily sobering and quieting effect of the methods which the Jewish exorcists practiced upon afflicted people. In either case the actual representation really is that any soul cannot endure anything but a vigorous life. The very humor of the picture especially in Luke points to the absurdity of the idle emptiness and makes the normally affirmative movement of the soul all the more apparent.

---

[6] Matt. 12:33-37.   [7] Matt. 12:43-45; Luke 11:24-26.

The parable of the sower has sometimes been understood in a fatalistic vein. The soul-soils are what they are. God made them so just as he made the varying features in the acreage of the earth. It is the sower and the seed and the cultivator that settle the actual results. Yet this is not all of Jesus' meaning. Either mainly or at least subordinately, Jesus means to teach vigor and activity on the part of the soil in its treatment of the seed. In the interpretation which the evangelists assign to Jesus the very point of the parable, its main teaching in fact, concerns the activity of the soil in making the seed germinate and develop "even a hundred fold." The semi-fatalistic interpretation of the parable may perhaps be connected with certain systems of theology which used to emphasize the passivity of the soul in receiving revelation, regeneration, and in fact every working of God upon the soul. In the thought of Jesus the human soul is intensely active.

Life along the lower lines is mere existence. Jesus considered such people as in reality dead, and said of them, "Let the dead bury their dead." [8] The prodigal son was "dead." [9] Men who were living in mirth and splendor every day, but at the expense of their spiritual life, such men as Dives or the prodigal son, might seem to themselves to be throbbing with the intensest life. In reality they had lost their souls because they had lost their higher life, and were in all strictness to be likened to a rich man who has indeed at last acquired unlimited wealth, but just as he reaches the summit of

[8] Luke 9:60.   [9] Luke 15:32.

his prosperity is stricken dead.[10] Thus in the native language of Jesus it was not natural for the soul to be merely receptive or merely neutral. It must be positively active. For the very word "soul" implied active life.

It was when some human soul poured itself forth in a full tide of thought, emotion, or act that Jesus was moved to make his most extraordinary statements. It was when Peter made his great and full confession that Jesus was the Messiah, the son of the living God, that Jesus declared that his Father had revealed it to him, and that upon such a character as he was then exhibiting he would build his impregnable church.[11] It was when Mary poured forth her whole soul and perhaps her whole fortune in the costly ointment, that Jesus made his extraordinary prediction that the story of her act should reach as far as the preaching of his good tidings.[12] It was when the poor widow gave all that she had that Jesus declared she had given not merely as much as any of the rich gave, but more than all of them.[13] Zacchaeus had been so heartily determined to see Jesus that he had climbed into the sycamore tree, had received him joyfully into his house, and had given his property, half of it to the poor, and the other half for making good to those he had wronged. Jesus declared that salvation had come to his house, and that he was a genuine son of Abraham.[14]

It is indeed true that each of these cases had its own

---

[10] Luke 12:16–21.   [11] Matt. 16:16–19.   [12] Matt. 26:13.
[13] Mark 12:43, 44.   [14] Luke 19:2–9.

peculiar worth. Yet they are so varied that we are led
to think that the total outpouring soul in its full
strength which characterized them all gave Jesus special joy because at these moments they all met, as it
were, his ideal of the soul. Their emotions and acts,
at least transiently, corresponded to the constantly
outpouring love and power of his own soul for men.

His words of grace at Nazareth declared that he
came to set at liberty them that were bruised. He proclaimed release to captives. It was the jubilee year for
mankind, a time for striking off chains and restoring
free activity for body and mind.[15] His feeling is illustrated by the case of the woman with the spirit of
infirmity. It was not her pain that moved Jesus. It was
her deprivation of the active use of her powers. She
needed to be untied and allowed liberty of motion. He
cut her thongs expressly that she might use her bodily
powers with freedom.[16] In the same spirit he sometimes set the soul of a sufferer free by his emancipating
forgiveness even before he removed the palsy from his
body. Miracles of mere display and exhibition of
power daze and benumb the soul. Jesus would not
work any such. But the restoration of man's normal
activities, as distinct from anything restrictive, he did
delight to achieve.

To Jesus' clear conception of the soul, as active, we
may add his interest in souls who were indulging in
careers of passionately active badness. In his story of
the shrewd but wicked steward he could separate the

---

[15] Luke 4:18 f.   [16] Luke 13:12, 15 f.

wickedness from the shrewdness and delight in the shrewdness even while he gave no expressed condemnation of the wickedness. In somewhat the same way he could sympathize with the various prodigals of his day who felt that life did not consist in repression but in expression, who sought with their whole souls for the thrilling sensations of a fuller life and, gathering all their resources together, plunged into the whirl of dissipation and the reckless self-expenditures of the passional life. No doubt these people were bad, but they were not the worst people in Jesus' world. For many of them went into the Kingdom of God while there was another class that stayed out. And they did have the somewhat redeeming quality of an energy and wholeheartedness that made them saveable.

There were in fact, speaking in reference to the soul as active, four classes of people. First, there were those who, like Peter, manifested an unrepressed outpouring goodness. Jesus loved them most. Secondly, there were those who led a consciously and genuinely moral life, which did not, however, make them self-sufficient but sent their hearts leaping upward toward something better. The rich young ruler belonged to this class. Jesus loved him not for the cold correctness of his moral life, but for his upspringing aspiration and eager heart which made him run swiftly toward Jesus and eagerly inquire for some diviner terms than he had yet known on which to inherit eternal life.

The third class consisted of those whose badness was active, enthusiastic, and full-blooded. Jesus had great hopes for these and brought many of them into the

Kingdom. For it was possible to separate their love of action from their badness and to direct its glowing stream toward the Father whose sons they were and who, if they would turn toward him, would meet them more than halfway. In modern therapy Anton Boisen tells us that in the mental hospital at Elgin the violent or active cases show a much larger percentage of cures than the apathetic, inactive ones.

There was a fourth class for whom Jesus had small hope. They had sealed up the fountain of life within themselves and sought to practice the same restrictions upon others. They were incapable of outflow. They had lost the natural activity which belongs to the normal soul. They had no real current of soul to be directed anywhere. What could be done for them? Their careers were finished. Jesus did not regard even *their* souls as inactive or their lives as unsuccessful. The only trouble with them was that their careers were finished. Their spiritual career belonged to the past. They had already, as Jesus repeatedly said, received their reward.[17]

Jesus' optimistic view of the saveableness of the soul is closely connected with his recognition of its essentially and normally active power. Being active it might turn toward God and goodness. Hence he did not despair of even the worst sinner. The very fact that a soul was plunging passionately along in evil made it possible that it should turn and plunge with equal passionateness toward the good. There was great hope

---

[17] Matt. 6:2, 5, 16.

for the energetic and conscientious Pharisee like Saul of Tarsus. He might become an equally passionate missionary. There was great hope for the woman in the city that was a sinner. She might get sight of him who forgave and from her forgiveness might result a passion of sacrificial love. There were those upon whose activities respectable custom and traditional procedure had settled "heavy as frost and deep almost as life." Jesus had his fears for these; for, the current of their normally active souls had lost its freedom by being sluiced into the confined and unbranching channel of their own selfishness.

Jesus' thought of prayer teaches the most intense and affirmative activity of the soul. The "pagans" thought they should be "heard for their much speaking," but mechanical endurance is different from spiritual activity. To pray is, according to Jesus, to put the understanding in motion. It is to concentrate thought upon one line. "Thy Kingdom come," says the model prayer. Even the supplication for forgiveness is immediately connected with intensely active forgiveness for others and made one with it in such a way that the soul cannot be in a merely receiving attitude but must be actively giving forth the thing it asks even in the very act of asking it. The model prayer is, after all, the prayer of a soul which has its own shoulder to the wheel.[18]

Subtle analysis of Jesus' teaching in regard to prayer sometimes is in danger of missing the mark. "Ask and

[18] B. W. Robinson, *Sayings of Jesus,* pp. 185–86.

ye shall receive" may be said to represent the "mystical mind desirous only of being a *passive* recipient of the light of God," but Jesus is really emphasizing the certainty that *active* and *earnest* prayer is the way to find the Father. The triple expression is for emphasis upon earnestness rather than analysis into variety of form. It represents the intensity of souls who know that their heavenly Father understands their material needs and, leaving the supplying of them largely to his care, give their whole souls to the Kingdom of God and the brotherhood of love.[19]

Whenever Jesus drew a picture of prayer the figure of the supplicant was marked by the same energy which he recognized and honored in actual life. The energetic importunity of the midnight visit for the three loaves of bread amounted to shamelessness.[20] The frequent coming of the widow to the unscrupulous judge was not a mere series of orderly calls. It represented an intensity of purpose.[21] Continuity and endurance may, like the much speaking of the heathen, be secured by proper machinery but the emphasis of Jesus is not on the patience that endures but on the energy that does not faint.[22]

The thing needful, then, in prayer according to Jesus' teaching is affirmative aggressive energy. But this demand is not an isolated or arbitrary teaching. It is in the highest degree natural to and consistent with his view of the soul and its Father. As a thing of

---

[19] Matt. 7:7–11; 6:32–34.   [20] Luke 11:8.   [21] Luke 18:2–8.
[22] Luke 18:1.

positive and fountainful power, the soul, if it prayed at all to its own Father, must pray with power, and the heavenly Father, as a corresponding fountainful and forthgoing love, would be sure to answer. The pure flame of love leaping up from the whole soul would be met by the descending flame of the Father's whole heart.

Jesus' teaching about prayer exhibits a remarkable antithesis. The Father in heaven knows what his petitioners have need of even before they ask him.[23] As his children they are to live in a spirit of unanxious trust. They are to have no fear even in regard to possessing the Kingdom of God, for it is their Father's good pleasure to give it to them.[24] Yet, on the other hand, they are to pray for the things they need with the greatest imaginable intensity. The antithesis is best understood in the light of the similar paradox which appears in the matter of becoming disciples of Christ. All men need do is to receive him.[25] They have received the good news and a place of membership in the Kingdom as a free gift.[26] But, on the other hand, the gift is not a material deposit. The soul is not a blank sheet or a "tabula rasa" which passively permits the divine message to be written upon itself. The nature of the message is such that it can really be received only by the most energetic grasping of it. There must be a positive and immediate commitment.

Matthew narrates that Jesus began to preach and to

---

[23] Matt. 6:8, 32.   [24] Luke 12:32.   [25] John 1:11.
[26] Matt. 10:8.

say, "Repent ye, for the Kingdom of Heaven is at hand." The repentance itself is active, as we shall presently see, but it is interesting to note that Mark's report has an emphatically affirmative additional note. "Repent ye, and believe in the good news." [27] Jesus' followers must do three things. They must forsake all they have. They must take up the cross. And they must follow him. The three acts are practically one. Yet it is important to note that the cross is not laid upon the shoulder of Jesus' follower but actively taken up by the follower himself; as Jesus' disciple the man does not stand still but "follows" him. The Kingdom of God, as Jesus brought it, seemed to be and was a gracious and rest-bringing gift. Yet the invitation to find the rest was coupled with taking the yoke.

How energetically Jesus conceived of the act of receiving the Kingdom appears with especial force when he uses the figure of his followers as "taking the Kingdom by storm." The Kingdom of Heaven is suffering violence and men are "impetuously crowding into it." [28] The picture of men of violence seizing a place by sudden attack portrays an energy of appropriation which may be separated in thought from the accompanying lawlessness and violence. Hence it is specially available when Jesus desires to exhibit the intense earnestness with which the Kingdom of Heaven is to be grasped.

The Kingdom of Heaven is to be received as a little

---

[27] Mark 1:15.
[28] Matt. 11:12; Luke 16:16 (Goodspeed Translation).

"child." [29] Here, too, the precise point of the comparison is important. To become a little child is not to lapse into a state of docility and incapacity, but affirmatively and actively to attain the glad, active, unhesitating energy and devotion of a child.

Jesus asks men to repent, but his use of the word is different from that of John the Baptist. With John it had a negative meaning. Soldier and publican must cease from violence and extortion. With Jesus repentance means "turning" from one condition or attitude to another. The good news of the Kingdom was being proclaimed. Jesus called men to change and "believe" it. A change of mind may take practical effect by making a man forsake evil courses or by making him turn to some new course of conduct or follow some new leader. The first effect is negative, the second affirmative or positive. When Jesus says, "Repent and believe the gospel," he does not mean to divide acceptance of himself into two stages but to indicate different aspects or different parts of the same act as, when in welcoming a new ruler, a city may remove obstacles and traffic from the street along which he is to come.

In brief summary God is not a being, sitting in repose upon a throne, but is a Father whose love flows forth toward all men like a mighty fountain. Man is not a being whose eruptive nature needs to be capped over and forced down but a being by nature expres-

[29] Mark 10:13-16.

sional, active, and fountainful like his eternal Father. In his very capacity for spiritual activity and force lies his salvation. Acceptance of Christ and his Kingdom is not in passive recipiency but in grasping with the total energies of the soul. Repentance is that change of mind by which the soul, in turning, brushes away any obstacles that may lie in the path of its movement. And faith itself is the whole soul, giving itself with its entire power to the open heart of God, as a returning son who has been a prodigal gives his whole being back to his father and finds that father's unlimited love poured back upon him. Acceptance involves an immediate and affirmative act of the soul in taking the gift, shouldering the cross, and pushing through the open door into the new brotherhood.

He who strives to preserve his own self will lose his soul, but he who loses himself in the gospel of love will truly find himself.[30]

---

[30] *Sayings of Jesus*, pp. 156-159.

CHAPTER X

Affirmative Goodness

IF THE special type of goodness which Jesus brought into the world consisted in an active outpouring of the good forces and qualities of the soul, his method of increasing goodness, that is, of making men better, must be obvious. He does not teach the lessening of the bad, at least not the direct lessening of it, but the increasing of the good. As the truly good man, whatever horror he has of evil, will have a still greater love for that which is good, so in seeking to become better, he will spend his main strength not on avoiding what is wrong, but on doing what is good—on doing as many spiritual things as possible rather than on doing as few fleshly things as possible. He will purposely and earnestly increase the outflow of goodness from his soul toward his fellow men. His ideal will not be to make his soul a garden enclosed so securely that no wild beast can possibly break in, but rather a producing territory sending out its fruits far and wide. He will not aim to be a sealed fountain from which no evil passion can possibly rush forth, but to be so closely connected with the high pressure of heavenly reservoirs that "from within him shall flow rivers of living water."

When, therefore, Jesus sought to help the young ruler he did not try to deepen or spiritualize his view of the moral law. The ruler claimed he had kept all the commandments from his youth. Jesus did not stop to carry the commandments inward and insist upon the guilt of hating a brother man so strongly as to wish him dead. He said nothing of the adulteries of the heart. In no way does he seem to have deepened the nature of the repressive work the ruler needed to do. For he saw that there was already a strong aspiration in his soul. It had some positive goings-forth already. Hence, Jesus sought to strengthen these and to point out a path of fuller action by inviting him to dispose of his property and use the proceeds for philanthropy, as a preliminary step to entering into the inner circle and more intimate service of the little company who had with affirmative resolve embraced the doctrine of the cross.

Jesus' highest word for goodness was life. He had little to say on avoiding death, but he had much to say on securing life, more life, fuller life, eternal life. In both the Jewish and the Greek world, virtue largely consisted in the control and subjugation of all bad passions and propensities. Jesus paid small attention to this restrictive discipline. He aimed at a state of mind in which all such passions and propensities were lost sight of or were consumed in the flame of an affection which set every faculty of the inner nature leaping heavenward and manward in love.

There has always been a large number of Christians who consider that the gospel demands a world-shunning and ascetic goodness. They build up their doctrine on the basis of the celibacy of Jesus and Paul and on many texts in the epistles which urge men to keep themselves "unspotted from the world" and free themselves from every worldly care. There are, they say, lower grades of Christian life which may, of course, be permitted, but this is the highest product, the counsel of perfection. But the conception Jesus had of goodness pictures a self-developing, soul-broadening force which was to remain in the world, live in it, and permeate it. "Increase your personal goodness," said Jesus. "Have salt in yourselves. Ye are the light of the world. Let your light shine."

In Stevenson's story of "Dr. Jekyll and Mr. Hyde" he pictures a man who had within him not only his regular self, the old Henry Jekyll, but also another self or character, a "wholly evil one." By swallowing a mysterious chemical mixture Jekyll became Hyde, and by repeating the draught, Hyde became Jekyll again. "The drug," says Stevenson, "had no discriminating action." It would work the change of character in either direction. The conception and the extraordinary popularity of this little book are full of suggestion. Such a low demonic self is thought to be almost natural. Given security from detection, men, it is felt, are capable of almost any evil.

In Plato's imagination when Gyges wears the ring, the turning of whose hoop or setting toward the palm makes him invisible, he does all manner of wicked things. The warning in Plato's and in Stevenson's pictures has no counterpart in Jesus' teachings. He sets before men a very different picture. They are children of God. He seeks to make them feel God's fatherhood as both a privilege and an obligation, and he does not set some incarnate devil before them as a demonic Hyde to warn them what a hell the heart may be, or a human life embody, but sets before them the perfect son of man and son of God into whose image they may be transformed. Jekyll's drug set the demonic element free, and gave it control. Jesus sought to give freedom to the higher self within the man. He was always wooing, stimulating, and winning men to the positive and full expression of the good that he saw within them.

In the light of the teaching that goodness consists in a positive power of love in the soul affirmatively asserting itself in the whole outward life, we are enabled rightly to estimate the relation of Jesus to non-Christian religions. The Golden Rule has been credited to Confucius, to Isocrates, and to almost all religions. They state the rule in a negative form which amounts to saying, "What things you do not like when suffered by yourself, do not do to others." The positive form of Jesus' principle [1] stands in sharp contrast to the negative rule of Isocrates.

In justice to Confucius and Buddha, it should be said that the lives of these men show that they meant to have their rule or teaching understood positively as

---

[1] Matt. 7:11, 12.

well as negatively. The real situation is clear enough. Anyone who starts out with the strong desire not to harm any living thing, brute or human, carries in that very desire a positive force which will lead him to do many affirmatively helpful and life-restoring deeds. And on the other hand, anyone who sets out upon a positive career of bestowing blessings and creating moral and religious life, and precipitates himself upon men with the absorbing purpose of giving them new life and giving it abundantly, may incidentally use some negative words even while his purpose of love keeps him from anything like physical harm to anyone. But when the first man, be he ancient or modern, speaking as a teacher, crystallizes the fundamental principle of his career into some sharply worded statement it will naturally take a negative form. On the other hand, when the man of purposely positive and affirmative career, speaking calmly as a teacher, crystallizes his fundamental purpose into a principle it will inevitably take a positive form.

Not to hide one's self from a brother's ox or sheep when it seems to be going astray but to bring it home and restore it to him [2] connotes in its mixture of negative and affirmative elements something very like the older attitude, while Jesus' teaching of the overflowing heart which does all things even to the enemy and the injurer which it would desire done to itself, connotes a love and life which have been raised to so much higher power that they practically constitute a new self-legislating spirit, beside which any partially nega-

[2] Exodus 23:4–6.

tive and partially positive rules for the mere details of
life, sink into secondary place.

It is worth noting that Jesus seems also to require a
specially *practical* quality in the goodness itself. There
are three things here: first, the fountain of a right
heart; secondly, the stream that issues from it; and
thirdly, the usefulness of the stream. It must not be
merely one which gives general refreshing and waters
the earth. It must become businesslike in a definitely
affirmative and practical way. An overflowing river
by virtue of its moving current has a positive quality.
But if it floats no ships and turns no mill-wheels it has
a certain negativeness, after all. Christian experience
abundantly teaches us that there may be a warm and
earnest heart which does not furnish power and light
at any particular point.

The businesslike quality of Jesus' affirmativeness
seems to add a further principle by making practical
requirements. All his parables and metaphors which
deal with the secret life of the seed or of the tree as
issuing in the grain and fruit of conduct, emphasize
the first two principles as we have just been giving
them. Goodness is an inward power necessarily pushing its inward life above the soil and along the ground.
But there is another set of parables which have the
third item, namely this strong businesslike tone. The
sound of trading in the market-place and of coin
counted into the banker's lap is heard in them.

No one can read the censure of the one talent man
and the one pound man for their practical inactivity,

or the commendation of the shrewd steward, without feeling the power of positive practicality in them. Laying up treasure in heaven, doing good and lending without hope of return, being polite in saluting not only one's brethren but outsiders and enemies, going the second mile, turning the other cheek to the smiter and many other similar sayings, while partly literal and partly spiritual in their intended meaning, are nevertheless so worded as to give the sense of a strong impact upon the practical items of daily life. They give, as it were, an additional push to the already active force of the Christian life and send it into the material provinces of ordinary human affairs.

We should avoid too great spiritualizing of the words that send the feast-giver's servants out into the highways and hedges for the lame, the maimed, and the blind. There is something more than the bare teaching of the rejection of the gospel by the Jewish leaders, or by the rich and learned in general, and its acceptance by the despised lower classes. There is a teaching in affirmative philanthropy also. We must beware of the negative attitude of waiting for these needy ones to come to us. The positive element in Jesus' picture is decisive against this and sends us out after them. To the inward force must be added the practical outflow and an affirmative business enterprise, as distinguished from the safe hoarding of the talent and the pound. The matters of philanthropic feeding and clothing of the needy come still more closely home to daily life. Jesus teaches an affirmative action which goes and hunts them up in their obscure retreats.

To this contention it must not be replied that we are building upon the mere imagery and drapery of a parable. For there are two opposite errors which are made in reading the figurative portrayals in Jesus' teaching. One tends to allegorize them completely. The other tends to take them altogether literally. It is hard to say which error is worse. The avoidance of both extremes lies in realizing the remarkable harmony between every part of Jesus' life and every other part and in the consequent further realization that the very imagery he uses, while not by any means constituting a stiff set of literal directions, does nevertheless carry and convey an idea of the kind of daily life he loves. This is because the pure, perfect, and complete outpouring of his soul embraced not only the teaching itself, viewed as abstract principle, but also the very imagery in which it was ensphered or crystallized.

Even in the great judgment picture in the twenty-fifth of Matthew we are not to say, on the one hand, that *mere* philanthropic care for the sick, shelterless, or imprisoned constitutes the direct basis of the final award, nor on the other hand, that these are mere details for which any other form of affirmative ministration might just as well be substituted. For they do reveal the fact that housing, feeding and clothing the poor, helpful visiting of the sick and imprisoned, and a hospitable heart toward strangers are forms of helpfulness especially dear to him.

Jesus' idea of goodness also requires unlimited forgiveness on the part of man toward his fellow man.

Peter sought a limit which seemed to him abundantly large. Jesus, however, extended Peter's "seven times" to seventy times seven. The parable of the forgiven but unforgiving servant, which immediately follows, reaches a severity of application which almost seems to make the pardon of the unforgiving impossible. Jesus, however, goes much further than forgiveness of one's brother man in general. He extends it to one's bitterest enemies. And lest the full tide of the forgiveness should be mistaken for a mere overlooking of offenses, he insists that the forgiveness of a brother man and reconciliation to him is important enough to interrupt worship or prayer,[3] and furthermore that prayer itself—and it must be sincere and earnest—include even a blessing for one's enemies and persecutors.[4] As the whole heart of the Father's love was poured out upon Jesus and as Jesus poured out his whole heart of love upon all men without exception, so he requires of his disciples that from their hearts they should pour out their whole inner being in forgiveness not only on those that came to them for forgiveness but upon those whom they have had to seek in order to effect a reconciliation and even upon those whose persecutions might seem to place an impassable gulf between the forgiver and the forgiven.

Men have sought to limit the forgiveness of Jesus by citing the unpardonable sin or insisting upon the palliatory clause uttered upon the cross, "They know not what they do," as though it were meant to restrict the area of pardon to ignorant transgressions. In paral-

---

[3] Matt. 5:23 f.   [4] Matt. 5:43, 44.

lel fashion it has been sought to limit Jesus' teaching of forgiveness by citing the ecclesiastical direction that after a certain amount of private conference and taking of testimony, the man who persistently refuses to listen to a brother's complaint should then be considered "as the gentile and the publican." [5] But the sin against the Holy Spirit is not, as such, a sin against an individual, and the impossibility of forgiveness is located in the nature of the sin, not in the heart of the forgiving God. In treating a man, after exhausting every effort to reach him, as a gentile and as a publican, Jesus, even at the severest, means no more than that such a man is to be regarded as no true member of the Christian society. Nor must we forget that treating a man as a gentile and as a publican must, in the last analysis, be interpreted in terms of that teaching which directs us to love, pray for, be courteous to and bestow substantial blessing upon the man who uses us worst, wherever he is.[6]

The special significance of Jesus' teaching on forgiveness, so far as concerns the positiveness of Jesus' doctrine of goodness, lies in the unfaltering power with which, having included every other and lesser department of ethical conduct in the tide of an outpoured love, he does not weaken its affirmativeness when directed toward the worst of men but, on the contrary, increases, if anything, the richness and fullness of the outflow in order to make it match the desperateness of the case.

---

[5] Matt. 18:15-17.   [6] Matt. 5:43-48.

In considering Jesus' teachings as to goodness we should naturally refer to the passive virtues. But the positiveness of Jesus, as we have conceived it, causes the passive virtues practically to disappear. The value of religion is not in its sedative properties. It is not an escape mechanism. Christianity has often been so depicted as to encourage quiescence or passiveness or even a mild fatalistic resignation rather than an aggressive and conquering force. The conception has certainly in recent years been greatly modified in favor of a more active one. Yet the passive virtues are still glorified much more largely than the teachings of Jesus will fairly warrant.

We may perhaps be making progress just now in attaining an important new stage in the history of human morality. The unlimited revenge sought by the passion of the primitive man was followed by the stricter justice of the law of an eye for an eye and a tooth for a tooth and no more. This in turn was followed by the idea of getting along peaceably with one's fellow men as far as possible. Out of this might be developed a kind of negative doctrine of non-resistance. Jesus, as we know, rounded out the history of goodness by restoring the unlimited overflowingness of primitive passion. Only he changed the overflow of revenge to the overflow of love.

In the practical working out of this conception we seem to be slowly entering into Jesus' teaching of the affirmative and active nature of goodness. If this is the fact it may account for the somewhat lowered estimate of the passive virtues and for the tendency to find a

more positive quality in them. The seemingly quiet
virtues may in reality involve great manifestations of
power. Humility, patience, and resignation may call
for the putting forth of greater energy than more conspicuous virtues. The power that causes a storm may
really be much less than that which reduces the elements to a great calm. Jesus' disciples themselves enter-
tained ideals of power quite different from those of
Jesus himself. They sought the twelve thrones of judgment and aspired to sit on the right hand and on the
left of the Master in his kingdom. Jesus' idea of power,
on the other hand, was power to bear suffering, to
shoulder the cross and push forward with it, to pour
out love in the face of prejudice and opposition. Yet
there was more positive power in Jesus' ideal and in his
life than there was in those of the disciples.

If we look at these so-called passive virtues in the
connections in which Jesus places them, the passiveness usually recedes at once. The good and honest heart
into which the sower casts his seed is not a merely
receptive soil. It is an active thing which is responsible
for the way it takes and treats the seed.[7] The beatitudes
are highly spiritual and have sometimes been thought
of as the headquarters of passive virtue. Yet they are
full of an affirmative power which is none the less because it is spiritual. The materialism of men's lives in-
fluences their material and physical conceptions of
positive power. Positive power, however, is positive
power, whether manifested in the cyclic storms of

---

[7] Matt. 13:19–23.

an astronomic nebula or in the quiet paleness and pleasant word of the man who is mastering an insult that touches the rawest and deepest place in his soul.

The whole subject of Christian suffering and self-denial sometimes seems to need restatement. Suffering has been too much glorified in and for itself. The healthy joyousness of Jesus saw no value in isolated pain or self-denial. He had no abstract teaching of mere "going without" things. The only things a man need go without were those which must be laid aside in order to go forward in the higher life. A soldier might take large baggage with him until the time came for the forced march or the impetuous charge. Then it might be necessary to throw away even his knapsack. There was no intrinsic virtue in "marching light." But if even one's entire wealth had become a crippling load it must be cast aside in the interest of a vigorous personal life.

Meekness is commonly rated among the passive virtues but with Jesus meekness is geared to extremely active achievements. The meek inherit the earth. Jesus' own meekness and retiringness are compaigning qualities instead of passive virtues. He does not strive nor cry, as we have seen, simply because not to be noisy or to advertise one's self is the best way to get ahead with the work of the Kingdom.[8] When he was silent before Caiaphas, Pilate, or Herod his silence was not the meekness of patient endurance but, like the refusal to strive or cry, was a very active and effective, though

---

[8] Matt. 12:16, 19.

calm, method of dignified self-assertion, as was abundantly evident from the irritation and surprise it caused.
When at the last he closed his life it is not said that
he died, or fell asleep, or ended his life, but the affirmative character even of his last hour is very clearly suggested by the statement: crying with a strong voice,
he said, "Father into thy hands I commend my spirit." [9]

It is sometimes said that Jesus not only recognized
a difference between active and passive virtues but
also delighted in meditative characters. Literature has
its active Jacobs who amass wealth and its meditative
Isaacs who go into the field at eventide. Dante has his
typical Leah and Rachel, and Martha and Mary have
been subjected to a like classification. But in the gospels Mary is not glorified for her quietness or because
"her eyes were homes of silent prayer." The good part
she chose consisted not only in household work but
also in sitting at Jesus' feet.[10] Martha's trouble was a
disproportion between the inward and the outward,
or rather in an overanxiety which took effect in outward overwork. Nathaniel was an Israelite without
guile, but his meditation under the fig-tree was not so
passive but that it led him to Jesus, and Jesus instantly
recognized not the meditative type so much as the
actively self-developing spirit which was destined to
see and richly recognize the communion of Jesus with
his heavenly Father. Goodness was never a merely
receptive characteristic but always expressive and pro-
ductive as well.

Spiritual "rest" is not for Jesus a passive quality.
It does not come by making slaughter in the streets

---

[9] Luke 23:46.   [10] Luke 10:39.

of Mansoul. Certainly it does not come by exemption from outward tribulation, for Jesus makes the tribulation and the peace go together.[11] The "rest" and the "yoke" also go together. The peace which Jesus gives is peace by empowerment, the vital peace of the elm tree whose high-arched branches rest upon the summer air, not the peace of the tree-timber which is dead and trodden under foot. Jesus does not disburden men but harmonizes the workings of their various powers with one another and with God. The unanxious trust which he enjoins is not a mere inward water of quietness where the heart rocks monotonously on the bosom of the great Father's love as idly as a painted ship upon a painted ocean. All this freedom from care is the resting of an airplane preparing for flight, or the steadying of its motion in its onward course, or the swooping to gain speed for the upward climb.[12]

Humility, again, is not a mere depressing of one's self to the lowest place. The humble man, in Jesus' teaching, does not put himself into a place of subjection or insignificance. It is active service that he seeks in the lowest place. Humility is reached by aspiration. Even though it is conscious of having attained the summit of some "heaven-kissing hill" it still is humble because its eye is upon the Alps, and if it had reached the level of the Rigi it would be lowly of heart because it saw the peaks of the Wetterhorn and knew of the Himalayas.

The ordinary doctrine of non-resistance is foreign to Jesus simply because it is set in a place of isolated negation. Jesus did indeed tell men not to resist evil but

[11] John 16:33.   [12] Matt. 6:19-34.

the saying has a setting. He does not tell men to endure all manner of evil meekly and do nothing about it. That would, indeed, be a doctrine of non-resistance. But he tells men when smitten on one cheek to turn the other also to the smiter. What he does teach is that we are not to be overcome by evil of any kind, physical, legal, or social, but are to turn about upon our enemy and attack him with whatever weapon of love, chance or providence may offer. It is as if Jesus had said, "Gird on your weapons of love and faith and assail your man with all your might. The evil man has played the aggressor. Do you likewise. But let your aggressiveness be the aggressiveness of beneficence." If this is the right reading of Jesus we must travel far beyond a mere doctrine of passive non-resistance in order to reach it.

In view of the passages in the Sermon on the Mount concerning purity of heart, on the one hand, and adultery in the heart, on the other, it need scarcely be added that the purity Jesus enjoined was passionate. Jesus and his early followers took purity in the comprehensive sense of the word. It meant a horror of everything that was unholy and a positive pleasure in everything that was pure, true, lovely and of good report. Purity of the body was of course included. But even this was not mere suppression of human instincts, but the sublimation of them in a new and affirmative direction. The spirit of God, according to Jesus, dwelt in man as in a temple. Jesus' idea of purity may perhaps be best expressed under Paul's conception. "Know you not," he said, "that your body is the temple of the

Holy Spirit which is in you? Therefore glorify God in your body." The single instance of absolute suppression of the natural instinct which Jesus mentions with approval is not a mere ascetic or negative self-denial but is achieved in order to reach the highest possible consecration to the Kingdom of Heaven.[13]

Jesus' teaching of toleration did not concern a passive or liberalizing virtue. Toleration for him did not consist in letting every form of belief and life go uncriticized because it seemed to be religious. His toleration was not of that negative variety which arises from vagueness and uncertainty of belief. It proceeded, on the contrary, from a positive conception of all good force and good work as essentially one. He would tolerate any irregularity of form in conduct and statement provided the man's essential mind and purpose were clearly and resolutely good. But the other side of this tolerance of every form of good was an intolerance toward evil. The first principle he expressed by saying, "He that is not against us is on our part." But as to the second principle, the principle of intolerance toward all definite evil, he said, "He that is not for me is against me." Once more we see the passive virtue in hand transformed into an intensely active one.

Watching and waiting for the coming of the New Day have often been conceived of as the consummate passive virtue of mere quiet expectancy. Its negativeness is often full of idle mischief.[14] But according to Jesus' conception the waiting and watching consist in

---

[13] Matt. 19:12. [14] See Tennyson's *St. Agnes Eve.*

a most intense activity of service and prayer. No fatalistic quietude nor even any strained but idle expectancy is imaged in the parable of the unrighteous judge.[15] We are apt to give to the idea of watching the somewhat negative aspect of men standing with loins girded and lamps burning, yet occupied not with any toil but only with tense expectation. In what the art of watching consists, however, is shown by the figure of the head servant who is busy providing for and ordering the duties of his master's household.[16] The parable of the talents is in fact Jesus' definition of the art of waiting. It consists in doing business for him and his Kingdom.[17]

---

[15] Luke 18:1–8.   [16] Matt. 24:45 f.   [17] Matt. 25:13, 14–23.

CHAPTER XI

The Negativeness of Moral Evil

JESUS' attitude toward moral evil is in line with his view of the nature of goodness as active and of the soul as an affirmative thing of life. Moral evil is the negation of good. We cannot say, however, that darkness is merely the absence of light or that badness is the mere negation of goodness, that "The evil is naught, is null, is silence implying sound."

There is a sense in which evil is a power for destruction like poisonous germs in the circulation of the blood or as tuberculosis in the lungs. Diseases are negative because they fight against health and their effect is the opposite of that of the vital powers. Yet the poison in the blood shares in its circulation and has much the same activity as the life-giving, life-carrying elements. In making promises, anything more than "Yea, yea," "Nay, nay" was wrong because it "proceeded from evil." [1] Murders, adulteries, fornications, thefts and all other forms of outward evil were the outflow of an evil source in the heart. [2]

Many peculiar turns of expression in Jesus' teaching

---

[1] Matt. 5:37.   [2] Matt. 15:19.

show his recognition of the active nature of evil. The unjust judge neither fears God nor regards man and says so frankly, at least to himself.[3] The prodigal goes to a country that is far distant and has his full fling.[4] Dives' robes are regal in color, and his linens imported from foreign shores. His banquets are sumptuous every day.[5]

Perhaps nothing more clearly shows this living activity which Jesus recognized in sin than his illustration of the evil eye. "If the light that is in thee be darkness, how great is the darkness." [6] The evil eye does not simply erase the real world. It creates another world within the soul where objects of all sorts are mirrored on the retina of the inward eye. The man who sins has a perpetual nightmare. His obsessed consciousness sees a host of strange objects set in strange juxtapositions. To him these objects are the veriest realities and he acts according to what he sees. The blindness of sin does not reach out a hand, like Elymas, for someone to guide it. Perfectly certain that its sight is good and with an air of complete superiority applying its blind organ to every object of vision in the whole landscape of life, it asks men, blind though it be, to conform to its ways and follow its leadership. Moral evil, then, for Jesus, spreads the shafts of its own blackness in every direction.

Jesus does not consider the life of the bad man as an inactive repose under his own vine and fig-tree. He, as well as the good man, is a builder. He builds on the

------

[3] Luke 18:4.   [4] Luke 15:13, 15, 30.
[5] Luke 16:19.   [6] Matt. 6:23.

sand, but he builds.[7] The selfish soul does not live a life of inactive ease. He has the whole world in view and seeks to gain it.[8]

The evil purpose of a bad man, moreover, not only impels his own career but that of others. The man who wrongfully puts away his wife makes her an adulteress.[9] There is much more here than the conception that putting away the wife indirectly leads her to adultery. Jesus' condensed expression does not stand for that. Through all the windings and complexities of her emotions, temptations, and acts runs the active force of her husband's evil deed in putting her away. The saying is true to human life. Through the devious ways of a man's unrighteous act there often winds the persistent force of some wrong done him by another, just as in an automobile or airplane power is often marvelously carried through a flexible conduit, however sinuously the conduit itself may be bent, and is active all the way to the very extremity. Jesus does not, of course, make the woman guiltless. He lets that question sleep for the time. He is dealing with the man and he wants him to know that his divorcing act is a force which "is and persists."

Some of the conventional religion was felt by Jesus to be a very resolute thing. It was not merely empty; it was misdirected. He expresses this by calling it leaven in distinction from bread. It is something which carries on a continuous and active work. Hypocritical teachers mixed their leaven with the meal of humanity

---

[7] Matt. 7:26.   [8] Matt. 16:26.   [9] Matt. 5:32.

and kneaded it in as thoroughly and persistently as the woman in the parable.[10] The intensity and peculiarity of Jesus' way of calling attention to this figure of speech implies as much.[11] Matthew omits the leaven of Herod mentioned by Mark.[12] Although professed Jews, the Herods sought to leaven Judaism with foreign customs. Their quiet and persistent activity in this direction is well characterized by the figure in hand. Jesus also characterizes some of the Pharisees and their work as a plant or planting.[13] The figure shows them not as a fixed and set organization but as a living and persistent growth planted in the land and constantly increasing its active influence and the corrupt fruit it produced. The underlying idea is much the same as when they are represented not as blind but as blind guides.

They also compassed land and sea to make one proselyte. Back of the hyperbole of Jesus really lay their actual and extended journeys to make proselytes.[14] Jesus noted and fully acknowledged the intense activity of their lives and how effective that activity was. The force of the new convert's change to Judaism co-operated in his life with the indoctrinating he had from some of his teachers to make him a worse Jew than he had been a Gentile.[15]

Covetousness had taken very deep root in some souls.[16] They were continuously adding house to house even though some of the houses were taken from

---

[10] Matt. 13:33. [11] Matt. 16:5–12. [12] Mark 8:15.
[13] Matt. 15:13. [14] Josephus Ant. 20:2, 4.
[15] Matt. 23:15. [16] Luke 16:14.

widows.[17] There was often a combination of covetousness with religious mistreatment. They said to men, in substance, "How was that oath of yours worded? It is money that talks. The temple is a great pile of stone. It cannot move or speak. But the gold in the temple is a living circulating medium. That is the vital thing to live and swear by. The altar of the temple is a mere sacrificial convenience. But the gift that is placed upon it represents the offering of the life to God. It is the sacrifice that is the sacred thing. If you did not put the word 'gold' or the word 'gift' into your oath, you need not pay the man you swore to pay. Give the money to us for temple maintenance." [18]

Nor did Jesus underestimate the success of evil on its own level in the world. The rich fool, Dives, and the shrewd steward are not represented as making a failure. Prevailingly, if not always, Jesus views bad men as succeeding in what they undertake. He does not tell of the financial breakdowns and failures of his rich men. The modern moralist has a way of saying: "You are aiming to get rich, to win praise or attain commanding position. Remember you are very likely to fail in your efforts. Why set your aim upon those things which perish in the using?" But Jesus does not speak in such a dialect. He has no pictures of men failing in business or in the ambitions of life. Jesus uses successful business in all his comparisons.

Jesus has no tale of a man caught on shipboard in a storm and losing his money or sinking with it in the

---

[17] Mark 12:40; Luke 20:46, 47.　　[18] Matt. 23:16, 17.

depths of the sea. He knows nothing of a career which ends in bankruptcy. The self-trumpeting alms-giver, the maker of ostentatious prayers, and the man who fasts to display his austerity are pictured as having attained the goals they sought. Over and over Jesus says of them, "They have received their reward." [19]

The more one reflects upon it the more striking it seems that a teacher who insisted upon the complete spirituality of goodness should have had nothing to say of the world as a cheat, of the broken health that so often attends the achievement of fame, or of the iridescent bubbles of every sort that are continually bursting and leaving nothing but the damp drop of disappointment. There are successes and successes. There is a higher success than some Pharisees achieve, a nobler reward than they have attained. But their success, such as it is, is a success, and the whole teaching is not a contrast between reward and punishment, but a study in success.

In Michal's appeal to Paracelsus her good angel does not bid her prophesy failure to him. No,

> He warns me not to dread a quick repulse,
> Nor slow defeat, but a complete success!
> You will find all you seek and perish so! [20]

Even the parable of the rich fool was spoken for younger men.[21] Jesus was not warning of sudden death. He was evaluating the success of the rich man and his long career of accumulation. What it illustrates

---

[19] Matt. 6:2, 5, 16.   [20] Browning, *Paracelsus* I, p. 26.
[21] Luke 12:16–21.

is the man that lays up treasure for himself and is not rich toward God. Jesus bids men make a study of successes in order that a lower success, however powerful and perfect, may not preclude a higher success which by comparison is related to the lower one as life is to death.

The great evil of sin, then, lies for Jesus not in the fact that it transgresses the fixed precepts of outward moral life or that it brings ruin and failure, but that it keeps man from entering his higher life, his true life. It is to be conceived of as a hand or foot whose activity is such that it pulls the man back from entering the gate that leads to a loftier career. The lower life which thus in any way acts as a thwarting agent upon the soul that otherwise would cross the threshold or enter the gate of a diviner existence is to be cut off.

In comparison with affirmative goodness, sin was essentially negative. This is the reason he gave to the various manifestations of sin no single or unifying principle such as he did find for all forms of goodness in the principle of love. However diffusive and penetrating the black rays of the dark light, they were, as related to the actual luminousness of eternal nature, a negative and privative thing.

Many Jews were devoted to decorative ceremonialism. They were strenuously devoted to sweeping and adorning. Yet the fundamental fact was that the sweeping and adorning were being done according to Jesus in an empty house.[22]

---

[22] Matt. 12:44.

The "publicans and sinners" who sat at table with
Jesus were doubtless guilty of many sins. Many leaders
desired the open castigation of such. John the Baptist
said: Let them cease from their extortions and rob-
beries. But Jesus did not view his essential work as
getting men simply to cease from doing evil. He chose
his metaphor with quick care. It is the sick who need a
physician.[23] These publicans by their very trade were
yoking themselves to the chariot of Roman oppression
and were helping to pull it vigorously along. Yet Jesus
thinks of them not as strong and resolute transgressors
of law. They are in bad health, sick and weak and in
need of a doctor. The very eruptions of the surface of
their lives, however conspicuous, revealed the defective and devitalized quality in the circulation of their
hearts' blood. It is his work as the great physician of
souls to restore their vigor.

Jesus has still another negative figure for sin. Not
only is the evil soul essentially without light, empty,
and diseased, it is also "dead." To the young man
whose father was in declining years and who expressed
the desire to postpone following Jesus so that he could
care for him in his remaining months or years and then
lay him reverently away in the grave, Jesus said in
substance, "You feel the stirrings of spiritual life. Your
father has enough other sons or relatives who are
spiritually dead. It may very appropriately be left to
them to care for those closing years and that burial. Let
no dilatory excuse slay the new life you feel. Come,

---

[23] Mark 2:17 et al.

follow me." [24] These other relatives of the man's father were doubtless active enough in their lives. Essentially they were dead. The Prodigal Son in his wild career of riotous spending was "dead." [25]

Thus the sphere and quality of evil men, as Jesus saw them in his deepest vision, were shadowy, anaemic, moribund, or quite dead. In reality their souls were "sicklied o'er" with a comprehensively and fundamentally negative "cast." Their activity itself consisted essentially in inaction. The evil of the things they did consisted, in the last analysis, in what they did not do. In the twenty-third of Matthew Jesus' lament over Jerusalem is not what we should have expected. It seems too tender and tearful to form a fitting climax to the preceding woes. It vibrates with disappointed love and prescribes a sad tone instead of an angry one for reading the whole chapter.

It is for want of shepherds that the people are suffering.[26] They had many guides and teachers but Jesus felt that they were unguided and untaught. Doubtless they were being led astray but Jesus speaks of them as though they were not being led at all. Even the saying as to the blind leading the blind seems to refer to some Pharisees as among themselves or to the fact that before judging others they must judge themselves.[27] Jesus everywhere seems to feel that the people of Galilee were in a negative condition in regard to the matter of having leaders. The very work which the Pharisees did with the commandments consisted in

---

[24] Matt. 8:21 f. [25] Luke 15:32.
[26] Mark 6:34. [27] Matt. 15:14; Luke 6:39.

nullifying their beneficent action. It "made them of none effect." [28]

The parable of the vineyard is directed against those who neglect their covenanted duty by not rendering the fruits when the season came for doing so.[29] The parable of the marriage feast is for those who will not accept God's grace when it is offered to them.[30] The same program of negation appears also in the excuses for not attending the great supper.[31] In the parables of the pounds and the talents it is not any embezzler or fraudulent character that receives the severe censure. The severity is visited upon the non-producers.[32] It is to these safe and careful do-nothings that the larger number of verses and the emphasis of the parable goes in each case. Even in the parable of the Prodigal Son itself the burden of the story is laid not on what trouble the younger son's dissipation brought him, but rather upon his failure to play the part of a son, and when he comes to himself it is his guilt and foolishness in staying away from his father that gets realization.

In view of all that has been said to establish the fact that the religion of Jesus is essentially positive it is evident that from the practical viewpoint the particular sins which Jesus rebukes would be prevailingly of a negative character. This is what we actually find. The sins which Jesus weeps over and scourges are "sins of omission," sins of not doing. To make the catalogue in detail would be mere repetition. A few instances will

---

[28] Mark 7:9, 13.   [29] Matt. 21:33-43, esp. 41.   [30] Matt. 22:2-10.
[31] Luke 14:18-20.   [32] Matt. 25:24-30; Luke 19:20-26.

easily set the reader's memory at work. The vineyard [33] where the husbandmen did not bring the fruit, the buried talent,[34] the pound in the napkin,[35] the servant who knew his lord's will and made not ready,[36] recall at once the staple quality of the wrong-doings mentioned in the gospels. They are in a word not wrong-doings but merely instances of not doing right.

Jesus said that Sodom would have repented. He also cites the case of Nineveh which actually did repent, and of the Queen of Sheba who did more and came from afar to hear the wisdom of Solomon. The sin of the men of Jesus' day lay in the simple fact that they would not receive him earnestly and honestly, that is, really and actively. The men of Nineveh had been guilty of no such neglect. The Queen of Sheba had traveled far in order to receive.[37]

It was the fruit which the tree did not bear which constituted its sin. This may be the explanation of the story or parable of the fig tree given by Mark. A fig tree had put forth leaves. Of course there would be figs hidden under them. But on examination there proved to be none. The out-leafing was an abnormal and premature pretense. On the morrow it appeared for what it was, withered as well as fruitless.[38]

Jesus was very patient with these lives that bore no fruit but if they persisted in their fruitlessness they would seal their own doom. This is the point of the fig tree story given by Luke. A practical owner might

---

[33] Matt. 21:33–41.   [34] Matt. 25:18.   [35] Luke 19:20.
[36] Luke 12:47.   [37] Matt. 12:38–42.   [38] Mark 11:12–14, 20 f.

cut down a fig tree that had been "fruitless for three years," but "one year more" and special care in cultivation might save it and Jesus was the vine-dresser who wanted even that fourth year for fullness of time and perfectness of effort to save. But after the fullest possible measure had been accorded, the unfruitful tree itself would have sealed its own doom.[39]

The man who knows his lord's will and does it not shall be beaten with many stripes while he that knew not and did things worthy of stripes shall be beaten with few stripes.[40] Anyone placed by God upon the height of knowledge, opportunity and power is on the verge of a correspondingly deep and enshadowed chasm into which he falls if he does not do the things which his knowledge, opportunity and power give him clearly to see as possible, needful, and dictated by the spirit of love. The great sin of the world, seen in the light of Jesus' teachings, is the refusal to adopt and receive the spirit of overflowing and active love to one's fellow men.

The sin of certain Jewish leaders, as far as concerned its bearing on themselves, consisted in their not entering the Kingdom of God. They also kept other men from entering it. That was the sum of their sin against their fellow men. The Kingdom of Heaven was a splendid and commodious dwelling. Its entrance, though straight and narrow, was spacious enough. But Jesus' enemies stood outside and while they would not go in themselves, they blocked the entrance so that

---

[39] Luke 13:6–9.   [40] Luke 12:47, 48.

other men could not do so.[41] The space in which they operated outside the gate was large and their ways of keeping men from getting to the gate were as active and manifold as the totality of their teaching and their influence. Yet shutting the door to others and preventing their entrance was the very essence of their sin as Jesus viewed it. The guilt which Jesus sees is the devastating of men's souls, the awful wrong of hindering God's little ones from walking in the new way,[42] the crime of arresting the new life, and of dulling the sensitive conscience.

Jesus' idea of sin may be briefly summarized. However true it may be from the philosophical viewpoint that the essence of sin is selfishness, Jesus does not seek to give it any unity except the unity of negation to the Kingdom of God. Sin is fundamentally a disease; it is the negation of spiritual health. Its superficial eruptiveness, however violent, is a sign of pernicious anaemia, of deterioration, and of death in the very currents of life. Modern preventive therapy knows the value of vitamins in building up immunity to disease through abundant health. A career of sin from the viewpoint of the good news which Jesus brings consists in the last analysis in *not* believing, *not* receiving, *not* doing, *not* promoting the things which belong to the Kingdom of God and the great Brotherhood.

---

[41] Matt. 23:13.   [42] Matt. 18:6.

CHAPTER XII

Examples of Positive Teaching

WHEN once the principle of affirmative action is recognized in Jesus, it gives larger significance to many of his more important teachings and attitudes. A few examples are here chosen in which our review of Jesus' positiveness may help to understand the deeper aspects of their meaning.

1. Jesus conceives of his mission as having the force of both "fire" and "sword." The very essence of his ministry is the promotion of peace and reconciliation of man with God and with his fellow man. Yet he conceives of this great work as throwing such an uncompromising force into the world, and as starting such a sweeping conflagration that only the resistless ravages of violent incendiarism and the slaughterous use of military weapons can furnish an adequate comparison. It is with the intensity of a fiery and wide-flaming heat that he has come to extinguish the flames of evil passion in the hearts of men. It is with the resoluteness of men who make war that he will bring his peace.[1]

---

[1] Luke 12:49–53; Matt. 10:34–37.

It should be carefully noted that Jesus' own power-ful sense of his mission is to be distinguished from the progressive stages in his announcement of it. The per-fect mathematician who knows the whole arithmetic may begin his tuition with examples in simple addition. This was Jesus' method. To the method of gradual in-struction must be added the practical restraints imposed by the already prevalent erroneous ideas of the Messiah and his work. Jesus could not announce himself as Messiah. It would raise too great a contrast, even in the minds of the disciples, between his evident low estate and the traditional pictures of the Messiah's might. Hence even when some work of mercy brought out a belief that he was the Christ, he enjoined silence as to that point.[2] He may even at first have felt that he could never accept the title. Little by little, and even quite fully in circumstances where it could wisely be done, he proclaimed his mission, until at the last he openly avowed it in the triumphal entry,[3] to the high priest at his examination,[4] and to Pilate.[5] In all this gradual revelation of Himself no careful reader will detect any lack of positiveness. The restraint which he put upon himself in the early stages of the training of the twelve in reality reveals the strength of his convic-tion. It is only a strong teacher who teaches nothing prematurely, but holds back that which will be wrongly understood and will confuse his learners' minds, if taught too early, until the time when it can

---

[2] Mark 8:30; Matt. 16:20.   [3] Luke 19:38-40; Matt. 21:15 f.
[4] Mark 14:62.   [5] Mark 15:2.

be safely proclaimed with force and clearness. When its time does come, however, the highest truth must be proclaimed with absolute plainness and, if need be, with unflinching courage. This is precisely what Jesus did.

2. In thinking of the Last Supper it is well to guard against negative or inactive ideas. Jesus views his death as a sacrifice and service which secures the emancipation of many.[6] It is one more recurrence of the keynote which he struck in his scripture reading from Isaiah at Nazareth. He was a great emancipator who came to proclaim release to captives, liberty to the bruised, and a jubilee freedom to the enslaved.[7] He viewed the woman who was bowed together as being bound by Satan and her cure as a loosening of the cords that held her captive.[8] Passages like these may serve to indicate the great emancipating force which Jesus not only saw in his general career but also in his giving of his life at last on the cross. Jesus went beyond the details of the passover celebration and, taking a cup of wine, declared that it was his blood, that is, his life, poured out in celebration of a new covenant, for many. But instead of pouring out the wine which was blood, or life, as David poured out the water which was the life of his heroes,[9] he bade the disciples, whatever instinctive momentary revulsion they may have had, to *drink* it.[10] There could scarcely be a more emphatic symbol or representation of the positive, affirmative, and life-

---

[6] Matt. 20:28; Mark 10:45.   [7] Luke 4:18.
[8] Luke 13:12, 15, 16.   [9] II Sam. 23:15–17.   [10] Matt. 27:27–28.

giving quality of his life and his death. He gave his life as a force which went into others and made them alive. It was not exactly or merely a shedding of blood. It was *blood transfusion*.

The Fourth Gospel shows this strongly affirmative view with special clearness. The brazen serpent saved men's lives, but the life of Christ not only keeps men from perishing but also bestows upon them "eternal" life.[11] The idea underlies the long discourse in the sixth chapter. The blood of Christ, i. e., his life-spirit, is the sole source of essential life. There is no other bread, and there is no other drink.[12] Some of the expressions in reference to the blood show that the death also is included as a method by which the life is bestowed. The grain of wheat falling into the ground gives rise to multiplied life. There is the picture of the universally attractive power of the cross, and of the going away of Jesus as the effective means of securing his universal, powerful, and spiritual return.[18]

3. Jesus introduced the "Kingdom of God." As Jesus' entire teaching in one aspect may be subsumed under the conception of the Fatherhood of God, so it may also be, in another aspect, under that of the "Kingdom of God." The expression had the advantage of being something concrete, yet at the same time large and mystic. It was a convenience for Jesus in carrying out his positive method.

---

[11] John 3:16. See especially B. W. Robinson, *Gospel of John* (Macmillan).

[12] John 6:27, 33, 35, 40, 44, 48, 51, 52–58.

[18] John 12:24, 32; John 16:7 et al.

He did not define this or any other terms in his teachings except by discriminating use. The Kingdom of God was not an external thing solely, for Jesus, nor an internal thing solely. It was divine love *in action* upon mankind. We have seen that Jesus set no value upon the outward, taken by itself, but rather made it the object of his irony. Nor did he value the inner condition of a soul viewed by itself. He could not think of goodness except as an inward light of love taking effect in outward life. This as well as the Kingdom of God, represented practically his entire teaching. The Kingdom of God is simply the divine power of love viewed as a force taking effect in ways as wide and varied as the life and history of mankind and of the earth it inhabits.

The teachings of Jesus in regard to the Kingdom are therefore all but innumerable. Jesus had a way of teaching one thing at a time. Hence the power of the Kingdom seemed at one time to be taking effect inwardly and at another time outwardly. At one time it belonged to the Jewish past, at another time it was among the men and in the men who surrounded him in his Galilean present. At still another time its dynamic quality was seen in some catastrophe or glorious transformation lying far ahead in the future. At one time it was an insignificant grain of mustard seed growing into a large herb. At another time it was a stone cut out of a mountain without hands, not, however, a merely quarried block, but endowed with a life that would make it fill the earth.

No definition of the Kingdom can rightly be made

which does not essentially incorporate this conception of a positive, affirmative, forth-going power. God was regarded in the Old Testament, as we have seen, in the light of both Father and King. But in the Old Testament the emphasis was so strongly upon the King that the Father was scarcely felt. Jesus, as we know, transferred the emphasis to the Father so powerfully that the King was scarcely felt. The same process he applied to the "Kingdom of God." It had been the rule of a righteous God in Israel giving external conquest and territory. The Jews, to be sure, often made the external conquest and territory the main matter. They wanted that first and trusted to its glory to produce inward and civic righteousness. The old prophets had, of course, viewed the matter more truly. They knew that inward righteousness increased and exalted the individual and the nation. Jesus' many teachings exhibit various forms of the one force just as truly as in the light of the scientific doctrine of the correlation and conservation of force all forms of force are seen to be differentiations of one inherent energy which is and persists.

A parable, for example, may begin by saying that the Kingdom of Heaven is like a man who did this or like a woman who did that. But Jesus never means to compare the Kingdom to a man or a mustard seed in and by himself or itself. What he means to say is that in the Kingdom of God, under such and such circumstances, things go as they do in the following story or process. It is the positive movement, the pervading force, the hearty and vigorous action, which he has in mind. When he tells a man that he is not far from the Kingdom of God, Jesus does not mean to say that the man is almost ready to join the church or to become a member of a restored and glorified Jewish theocracy. He means that the movement of the man's mind and thought are approaching that quality of *forth-going love* which embodies the true conception of the Kingdom.

There is a modern use of phraseology which gives an impression of the Kingdom as a fixed and static thing. It is thought of in terms which inevitably suggest an external society of enrolled men and women into which one may be admitted on certain terms. One feels that a force which, as a force, is forever in motion has somehow been measured and crystallized. It may of course be replied that Jesus himself used similar language when he spoke of entering the Kingdom of God. But whoever will read at one sitting all that Jesus has to say of the Kingdom of God will find himself just as he finds himself in the world of nature and of human history, in the presence of a force which is acting in a thousand ways and producing a thousand effects, but is itself, after all, and however intricately and variously differentiated, a force and an energy, nevertheless. What it may produce in the future no man can tell, any more than he can tell what the cosmic force of the sun may yet produce in the way of transforming the earth. The man who believes in the Kingdom of God as divine love outpoured in effective action may reasonably expect in the future results of all sorts too rich to describe.

4. Jesus is positive in his attitude toward the use of property and money. He does not regard poverty as a blessing. Renan asserts Jesus' lofty and ironical disdain and even scorn of earthly things.[14] He says rather, "Change your money into spiritual treasure. Transmute it into heavenly credit. Provide for yourselves bags that wax not old, that do not have holes in them." [15] In this positive treatment of property and money Jesus is more positive than many great thinkers.

In regard to educating the guardians and controlling spirits of his ideal Republic, Plato says, "As for gold and silver we must tell them that they are in perpetual possession of a divine species of the precious metals placed in their souls by the gods themselves and therefore have no need of the earthly ore, that in fact it would be profanation to pollute their spiritual riches by mixing them with the possession of mortal gold, because the world's coinage has been the cause of countless impieties, whereas theirs is undefiled: therefore to them, as distinguished from the rest of the people, it is forbidden to handle or touch gold or silver or enter under the same roof with them or to wear them on their dresses or to drink out of the precious metals." [16]

Of the people of Utopia, More says that "of golde and silver they make . . . vesselles that serve for moste vile uses not onely in their common halles but in every man's private house. . . . Finally whosoever for anye

---

[14] Renan, *Vie de Jesu*, pp. 123–124.   [15] Matt. 6:20; Luke 12:33.
[16] Plato, *Republic III*, 416, 417.

offense be infamed, by their ears hange rynges of golde. Thus by all meanes possible they procure to have golde and silver among them in reproche and infamie." [17] This negative note of lofty scorn and disdain is entirely absent from Jesus' teaching.

Not that money does no harm. Riches do make it hard for men to enter the Kingdom of Heaven.[18] Jesus showed the rich young man how to enter into life. He told him to sell all he had; and give to the poor.[19] Jesus did no despite to the money as money, but under the circumstances it was, for this particular individual, a hindrance, and the use of it for the poor a way of life.

It was with the same reference to spiritual life also that Jesus said in substance to the avaricious brothers, "Covetousness is contrary to a man's true life, and covetousness may flourish in the frigid climate of poverty as really as in the tropic zone of possession. Therefore for this reason, namely, that it keeps you from your true life, I say to both of you, Beware of it." [20] It is because men cannot give their lives supremely to two things and because God is supreme, that Jesus bids men not to be anxious to the point of "worry" in regard to the means of subsistence.[21]

Jesus' objection to riches was in the interest of that pure and positive spiritual life which was his great aim for men. But such a life was to be nourished, it should be especially noted, not simply by parting with money and property, but by using them in the right way.

---

[17] More's *Utopia*, Book II.   [18] Matt. 19:23 f.   [19] Matt. 19:21.
[20] Luke 12:13–15.   [21] Matt. 6:25.

Jesus does not follow the fashion of Plato and More by saying, "Get out of sight of the filthy lucre and get it out of your sight, for it is vile." He says, though in his condensed fashion, "Open up your heart in sympathy to the poor. They are all about you. Pour out your money and your affection upon them to the uttermost. This is my test. Can you meet it? If you can you will have the kind of soul that can come into my company." "Money in itself," said Jesus, "is perishable, but it may be transmuted into something eternal. This perishable money of yours may be laid up in heaven."

Jesus made men understand how such a thing could be done, by telling his story of the shrewd steward. That quick-witted individual with fine foresight did a good turn to his lord's debtors in order that when he was discharged he might be received into their homes. Jesus applied the story of the steward by saying, "Use the mammon of money to make to yourselves friends in the spiritual world." [22] The story of Zacchaeus points in this same positive direction. Zacchaeus when he is converted takes his money and sends it forth in practical and systematic restitution and beneficence.[23] It is the positive use of money to promote the growth of his kingdom of brotherhood which connotes Jesus' essential, if not his entire attitude in regard to it.

5. The Sabbath was made for man.[24] Jesus also added that man was not made for the Sabbath. He had

---

[22] Luke 16:9.   [23] Luke 19:8.   [24] Mark 2:27.

good reason. For the scribal regulations had put so thick a hedge around the law of the Sabbath as a negative institution that they practically made the field of that commandment all hedge and no law. The tailor must not take his needle with him toward dusk on the Sabbath eve for fear he should forget and carry it after dark on the holy day. When the scribe went out at the same hour he must not have his pen behind his ear. He might forget to lay it down as he watched the stars come out. A cripple might, but again he might not, keep his wooden leg on during the sacred hours. Two thousand paces was the limit of a Sabbath day's journey. If Jesus' disciples rubbed out a few heads of wheat on the Sabbath they were guilty of threshing. If the healed paralytic used his new given strength to carry his pallet it was a profanation of the sacred day.

The positive handling which Jesus gave the Sabbath becomes evident when we observe the exceptional nature of the passages which, in defense of his disciples and himself, he quotes from the Old Testament. David's eating the shew-bread when fleeing from Saul,[25] the priest's kneading the oil into the meal-offering,[26] do not represent the general trend of the Jewish law. Jesus erects these peculiar exceptions into a principle broad and general. The Sabbath is not a negative something to be kept untainted and unbroken. It is a positive means for affording refreshment and doing good.

The Sabbath, as Jesus found it, was a grand old structure full of closed and forbidden rooms. It was a

---

[25] I Sam. 21:6. [26] 7:12.

castle belonging to an absent lord as exclusive pro-
prietor. The paid servants were admitted to its halls,
because they were essential as defenders or caretakers
who looked after its dignity and up-keep. Jesus per-
emptorily assumed possession and authority in the
premises and then dedicated the whole property to
the use of the people forever as a public domain to be
administered in the service of humanity. The right
"law" or principle for the observance of the Sabbath is
to consecrate it as a day on which "to do good" and "to
save life." [27]

6. It is by reference to the positive quality of Jesus'
own character, teaching and spirit that we rightly understand his idea of men's final destinies. The final
destiny of the good is essentially affirmative. The final
destiny of the bad is essentially negative. Jesus' whole
personal consciousness was one of positive outpouring
love. That was his blessedness. That was his essential
heaven. To miss it would be the greatest punishment.
Just as he finds the essence of all goodness in love but
names no essence of sin, so he finds the essence of his
heaven in love while the essence of his hell is negative.
It is the absence of love. As his contrast between good
and evil men is, in the last analysis, a contrast between
those who do good and those who do not do good, so
the destiny of the one class as contrasted with the other
is not, as he views it, the contrast between being in
heaven or in hell, but the contrast between being in
the Kingdom and being outside of it.

When the lord returns and enters upon the joy of

---

[27] Mark 3:4.

his returned life he bids the faithful man to enter into
and share his joy. The unprofitable servant, however,
is simply put out into the dark.[28] There is weeping
and gnashing of teeth outside the palace. But it is a
weeping and gnashing not because of any tortures that
are being inflicted upon the outsider. It is because he
is outside. The bitter lot of the five foolish virgins
consisted not in stoning or imprisonment but in the
fact that they did not get in to the marriage. The loss
of a soul for Jesus is the loss of what it might have been.
Its punishment is not in torture but in perishing.[29]
Judgment is elemental, not personal, except as the personal and the elemental coincide. It is the words that
will judge at the last day.[30] It is not the preacher of the
Sermon on the Mount but the rain storm that will
decide the hearer's destiny.[31] The real punishment of
Jerusalem was in missing her opportunity.[32]

The great judgment scene in the twenty-fifth chapter of Matthew is highly significant in connection
with the positiveness of Jesus. The setting of the scene
is so magnificent that every theorist of final things
has claimed its grandeur to adorn his scheme. How did
Jesus himself see it all as he pictured it? What were
the contents of his consciousness as he outlined its
terse and telling imagery? Did he think of the apoca-
lyptic throne of woven wind and cloud as a thing
that would come *literally*? Were the angels and the
nations to be there in localized ordering and occupied

---

[28] Matt. 25:30.   [29] John 3:16.   [30] John 12:48.
[31] Matt. 7:24-27.   [32] Luke 19:42, 44.

mileage of space? Let us rather ask, "What is the great principle of decision which lies at the heart of this scene whose simplicity of vital power will not let it die but gives it eternity in men's hearts and consciences?"

The judgment turns upon the presence or absence of humane activity toward any of God's children. The Son of Man passes no sentence for robbing the poor of bread, for poisoning the enemy's wells, or for hauling men and women into the fetid air of undeserved and deadly dungeons. He simply sees a brother at the hunger point, or unclad, or sick, or behind the bars. Over against that figure he sets the man who gave and the man who neglected to give the food, the shelter or the succoring visit. It would seem as if Jesus might have painted the contrast with a far more effective brush. He might have set on the right hand those who had given to his disciples glad hospitality and generous support and on the left hand those who had beaten them with rods, crucified them, or sawn them asunder. But Jesus simply contrasts those who have done the acts of humanity with those who, like the priest and the Levite in the parable, have gone by without doing them. The mere and bare presence or absence of positive and affirmative kindness is erected into a touch-stone for eternal verdicts.

CHAPTER XIII

Positive Action

THE beneficent deeds of Jesus were acts of brotherly helpfulness. For Jesus did not believe in a merely distant God. He believed in a near and present Father who took care of grass, sparrows, sunrises, rain, and men. He was giving his life to the exhibition of God as just such a tender and compassionate Father. That was his prime mission. It was simple fairness and consistency that his deeds should be like his character and like his teaching. It was a moral impossibility for him to raise any rock-breaking whirlwind at any Horeb or to cause the earth to shudder with earthquake.[1] His work was essentially one with the constant elemental life-giving and restoring powers of nature.

If we had before us today every man upon whom Jesus used his power and looked at him as he was after Jesus was through with him there would be nothing very noticeable about him. We should need to be told that this man had been blind, for he would be looking out of his eyes like every other man. We should need to be told that that other man had been deaf for he

[1] I Kings 19:11 f.

would be hearing our speech as other men do. We should need to be told that this third man's hand had been useless for he reaches it forth and with it cordially shakes our own. Jesus healed great numbers of sick, palsied, maimed, and lame. The number of detailed individual cases, as seen in the lists of his deeds, is a very considerable one. We are told in the gospels of large numbers being healed at the same time.[2] Here is a woman walking healthily along. You have to be told that previously she had been bent together and "tied fast" in that position "by Satan." [3] Here is a man whose vital powers are being drowned out by dropsy.[4] Jesus heals him and lets him go. Here is the daughter of Jairus. She has been dying on her bed. Now she is up and hungry and should have something given her to eat.[5]

The quality we are impressed by in all these stories is their affirmativeness. There is not an act of destruction among them. Anyone who will set an ordinary list of the Old Testament miracles beside the works of Jesus will be struck by the contrast. In Jesus' list there is no Gehazi or Uzziah smitten with leprosy. There is no Jeroboam with a withered hand. There is not a drowning or a death stroke. Jesus alone stands forth in the scripture between prophets and apostles as the great worker of unvarying and positive beneficence. He never harmed so much as the hair of any man's head. There was a fig tree that had departed

---

[2] Matt. 14:34–36; 15:29–31; 19:2. [3] Luke 13:13. [4] Luke 14:4.
[5] Mark 5:43.

from nature and though leafy was essentially dead. In the story Jesus made its real condition obvious as a parable or picture of the condition of individuals he loved too well to visit upon any one of them the slightest actual harm. In the story of the Gadarene demoniac the swine which drowned were not thought of by the Jews as having such value as an American farmer might ascribe to them.[6]

Let us imagine three houses standing near each other. The first is the home of those persons who have been wrought upon in early primitive wonder stories. Here is Naaman the Syrian with skin healthy as a child's.[7] Around and about are a great multitude of those who have been fed with manna. Not a few of them have been bitten by deadly serpents but they have looked at the brazen serpent and are alive and well. But in this strange house Nadab and Abihu lie dead with bodies marred and burned by the Lord's avenging fire. Here are two score and two children that have been torn by bears. Here also are two men, a servant of a prophet, and a King, covered with the white death of leprosy. Outside there where you see, through the window, the freshly disturbed earth, Korah, Dathan and Abiram have been swallowed up alive. Out there on the edge of the grounds are the blackened bodies of complainers upon whom the fire of the Lord has gone forth at Taberah. There are men in this house who have been delivered from the lion's den and saved

---

[6] Matt. 8:29–32. See Dibelius, *From Tradition to Gospel*, page 89.
[7] II Kings 5:10–14.

from the wrath of the sea. But an innumerable company of dead lie outside, including even the smitten host of Sennacherib.

Passing by the second house for a moment, we come to the third. Here is a man who if you will listen will tell you a story of having lain lame at the Beautiful Gate of the temple. Here too is a woman quite happy and wearing a kindly smile. She has a needle in her hand and is making garments for the poor. For Peter has raised her from her bed of sickness and death. But here, as we pass through a door into another room, is a man who is groping about in blindness "seeking someone to lead him by the hand." His enmity to righteousness and his perverting the right ways of the Lord have brought him to this pass through the effective judgment pronounced by Paul.[8] And still farther on in a darkened apartment lie the bodies of a man and his wife who in an hour of general consecration of property have lied to the Holy Spirit and kept back part of the price of their land. For Peter has pronounced judgment upon Ananias and Sapphira and they have fallen dead.[9]

With a saddened, even if justifying, heart we turn back to the middle house, the house of the Son of Man. Remembering what you had seen in the other two houses you hesitate to enter this one. Some awful sight will break the new-found, wide-ranging charm of perfect health and unexceptional vitality. Yet you

---

[8] Acts 13:9-11.
[9] Acts 5:1-11. For Luke's love of "punitive miracle" see Cadbury, *The Making of Luke Acts.*

cannot hold back. You enter the door. Here is a young girl who meets you laughing with health. She had been sleeping what her friends called the last sleep. But that is overpassed. Here are a company of fair-complexioned men. They had been lepers. All through these rooms are those who see and hear and sing, those who had been tossed in the delirium of fierce fever, those who had shaken with the palsy, and those who had suffered with nameless and hidden disease. With beating heart you go from room to room. You see its every occupant. It exhibits the objects of the power of Jesus as they were when his work upon them was completed. There is no sufferer curtained off in any smallest alcove. There is not even the skeleton of a child in any closet.[10]

Can any fair-minded man fail to read the lesson of the life and work of the Nazarene? He came to pour out upon men a heart of perfect love which was the revelation of that God whom he called Father. He came to bring every man into perfect health and activity like his own. He was the normal man and he wished to conform the abnormal children of men to his own image. His life was the fullness of the outpoured positive and affirmative. Every human being upon whom his grace and power took effect was made whole, active, and, so far as they would receive his grace, a power of outpouring purity and beneficence like himself.

---

[10] For destructive stories about Jesus in later literature, see M. R. James' *Apocryphal New Testament*.

The profound and perfect harmony which subsisted between Christ's teaching and his works makes them object-lessons of the spiritual effects he aimed to produce and often actually did produce later among his followers. The whole apostolic age is full of these effects. In the Acts and Epistles there is the most abundant evidence of a free and empowering spirit in the hearts and lives of the apostles. It was a spirit which handled the Sabbath with nearly as bold and firm a hand as Jesus himself, a spirit which, like his, gave Old Testament passages larger and more positive meanings than their original writers intended and even turned the patriarchal history into allegory where that would serve to enforce the spontaneous and continuous freedom of the spirit of Christ in the soul. It was a spirit which handled Jewish ceremonial with an astonishing liberty. It saw no difference whether a man were circumcised or not. If narrower souls said the rite was necessary, it entered a denial. Uncircumcision like circumcision was nothing. It was a spirit which, like Jesus', assumed the necessity of moral purity in the fullest sense of the words, but laid no special stress upon the negation of gross sin and reserved special urgency for enforcing the affirmative walk in the spirit. "Live by the spirit and then you will not indulge your physical cravings." [11]

What is more natural than that the life of the apostolic age should exhibit a similar, free, self-legislating, positively self-affirming, spirit? It was a case of con-

[11] Gal. 5:16.

tinuity. When once we grasp the fact that the positiveness of the gospel, in the sense in which we have tried to explain it, is its deepest and most pervasive quality, it need not surprise us that Stephen's face wore a radiant expression before the Sanhedrin [12] or that Paul and Silas sang hymns at midnight in the inner prison at Philippi.[13]

The majority of the men of Jesus' day did not, of course, understand him at all. But there were some among his disciples whose experiences as companions of Jesus during his ministry added much to the light which the resurrection later cast upon them. They were able to appropriate the peculiar affirmativeness of Jesus so strongly as to send the new religion onward with power. We cannot explain the new start which Christianity took after the resurrection by a mere reference to the resurrection as a vindicating of Christ's character. We must give equal and even especial prominence to the positive, outpouring, forthgoing, onmoving character which it vindicated.

One author speaking of the positive side of veracity says, "Had the disciples of Christ, after the death of the Master, merely refused to deny him directly, had they returned to their former callings, and, obeying the commands of the authorities and the dictates of prudence, locked up the memories of the past in their own hearts, they would surely never have become what they now are: witnesses of the truth, whose testi-

---

[12] Acts 6:15 cf. *Tennyson Two Voices*, pp. 219–225.
[13] Acts 16:25.

mony is shaping the destinies of the centuries." [14] But what was it which gave them the courage, the active and effective courage to be the strenuous witnesses they actually were? Simply the fact that the most inherent and deep-seated quality of the very message they had in their souls was such a forth-flowing, out-speaking, help-giving positiveness that the very act of keeping their Master's teaching quiet or even of being negatively faithful to it by admitting it when questioned would have been a self-contradiction in their own souls and would have killed the truth they cherished. The apostles proclaimed the gospel of Christ because for one reason proclamation was just as essential to the very quality of the gospel as a mountain-stream is to the lofty spring from which it starts.

Jesus was always seeking, not to destroy the evil in saveable souls, but to enhance the good in them. He seeks, in other words, to carry their positive aspiration up to a higher point, transforming it on the way thither. Jesus in fact treated the individual as he treated the Jewish law. He fulfilled the man's better part. The fulfilling might do away with not a little that the man had cherished. That, however, was incidental. The method itself was to fulfill, to impart new life to what was already present. There was an increase of vital power in the whole man but especially at the point where the particular need had existed. The spring of

[14] Paulsen, *Ethics*, Eng. Trans. 685 f.

good in the man had been increased to a fountain, the rivulet to a river which, after the manner of rivers, purified itself as it flowed on in the sunlight.

The *foreigners* whom Jesus reached did not find themselves turned into Jews as a necessary preliminary. The Roman centurion had a military view of Jesus' authority. When Jesus left him, his militarism had not been chastised but elevated. His particular form of faith had been glorified even at the expense of the Jews themselves of whom Jesus was one.[15] When the woman of Samaria had been transformed by his teaching she had not been compelled to abjure her native ritual. Her water pot had been filled with meanings so large that she forgot to fill it with water. The ignorance of her superstition had been enlarged to the knowledge of a spiritual faith and her narrow service widened into a missionary effort. But there had been no direct and violent breaking down of her old ideas, nor any denunciation of her life. The human yearning for God had been developed to its fullest possible capacity. She began at a local well and traveled all the way to the belief in the Savior of the world.[16] But the road was not made by crushing down the wrong protuberances of her thought and life so much as by taking advantage of its elevations for constructing a highway. Nothing in the whole story affects us so much as the fact that Jesus did not utilize his opportunity to excel in the fine art of excoriation but found even in such a woman something which he could build

---

[15] Matt. 8:5-13.   [16] John 4:7-42.

up into eternal life. He gave her no flashes of the judgment day such as John the Baptist was wont to give.
There was some good in her. When he left her there
was much more developed out of it.

He let the thankful leper go at the same time that
he called to his consciousness, not his foreign nationality nor his unclean life of disease, but the real faith
which had saved him.[17] The Syro-Phoenician woman
did not belong to the lost sheep of the house of Israel;
but Jesus did not compel her to become a proselyte,
nor did he reproach her for the undeveloped character
of her faith. He praised her for the spiritual force with
which she extended his metaphor of the dogs, and
bestowed the healing of the Nazarene upon the
Greek.[18]

Paul's universalism refused to put any Jewish bar-
riers between any Gentile soul and Christ. The direct
accessibility of God for men of every nation he declared by exhaustive lists of nationalities and conditions
of life. He also recognized that those who, not having
the law, did by nature the things contained in the law
showed by that very fact that they had the larger law
of conscience written in their hearts.[19] Jesus' universality appears in the biographical fact that he recognized genuine faith wherever he found it. If one had
to choose between the extensive universalism of Paul
and the intensive universalism of Jesus he must, I think,
prefer that of Jesus. For while Paul reaches his wide-
ness by a far-traveling range of thought and life, Jesus

---

[17] Luke 17:15-19.   [18] Mark 7:24-30.   [19] Romans 2:14 f.

reveals his by the quiet power which recognizes the
direct power of faith in foreigner and Jew alike, and
extends his saving power to the lowest ranks of society.
It is the universalism of unlimited love as distinguished
from the universalism of cosmopolitan travel and fully
developed religious philosophy. Jesus' directly positive
method took an outside or foreign faith just as he
found it and enhanced it and strengthened it along its
own line and left it the same but strengthened and
empowered.

The affirmative method of Jesus, as applied to his
own disciples, is here full of interest. Peter's ambition
looked upward. He felt that his abandonment of everything in the interest of Jesus deserved recognition.
What was he to have? On the basis of a Jewish theo-
cratic kingdom there was to be a separate throne in
each of the twelve tribes. Each apostle was to have a
throne and administer its splendid new conditions as
chief executive.[20] Rightly understood, it is another
good example of Jesus' affirmative method. The apostles were the best men of their day. They were at least
the best available to Jesus. Jesus did not crush their
ambition. He told them it should be fulfilled.

It is true that in the act of telling them so, he gave
their conception a transforming uplift. Sometimes he
raised questions which would set them to thinking.[21]
Sometimes he made use of a gentle irony. Sometimes
he drew the extremely antithetical picture of an ethical
monarchy founded upon sacrifice and service.[22] But

[20] Matt. 19:28.
[21] Matt. 20:22 f.   [22] Matt. 20:25–28.

he never directly annihilated, scourged, or even chastised an existing ambitious conception of his disciples. For the dross in their hearts was mixed with much gold. The still garden of their souls was growing more wheat than tares. They had more saline matter than earthly in the total solution of their characters. In the fusing heat of love the dross could be refined away. When wheat and tares had grown together till the ripening harvest time the tares could be cast away and burned. In due time the earthly sediment would settle and the saving salt would crystallize apart by itself. Therefore, Jesus gave special attention and increase to the gold, cultivated intensively where the wheat was thickest and constantly made the salt more pungent, added to it from his own store and put it on the way to more rapid crystallization.

When Peter accepted him as the Christ, Jesus proceeded without preliminary refinements or deductions to picture his all-conquering church as being built upon just such a personality as the apostle was then and there exhibiting.[23] The rebuke that came a little later was sharp enough and destructive enough, but that had nothing to do with the building up of Peter's constructive conception of the Christ. The later rebuke was solely in the interest of another positive conception, the teaching of the cross.[24]

In studying Jesus' training of the twelve, then, we need have no difficulty with those statements which seem to lack spiritual quality or even to point to material conceptions and to material rewards. For Jesus,

---

[23] Matt. 16:16-19.   [24] Matt. 16:22 f.

finding his man moving along the ground simply increases the man's speed and at the same time lessens his downward pressure upon the earth by providing him with motor and wings of higher ideals, until at last he gets clear of it altogether, takes to the air and continues his motion in that loftier element.

But it may make the affirmativeness of Jesus' work still more clear to observe a few more examples. Zacchaeus was a social outcast with whom no self-respecting Jew would sit at table. He had acquired the things which it is possible for wealth to have. He had a fine home, doubtless, filled with the best appointments and service of the day. One thing he missed. Reputable Jewish citizens would not seek his mansion and he could not break into good society. Jesus recognized his ambition and the saveableness of his soul. With conspicuous publicity he took social recognition to Zacchaeus' house, restored him with emphasis to his social position as a "son of Abraham" both by birth and re-birth and by this affirmative building upon Zacchaeus' own social desires carried his life to the altar of a redeeming faith on which his property was dedicated for restitution and for benevolence.[25]

No one who knows Jesus' affirmative spirit can fail to be impressed with his treatment of the woman with the issue.[26] Modest shame and concealment were preying upon her and she had superstitious faith in a fringe.

---

[25] Luke 19:1-10.   [26] Mark 5:25-34; Matt. 9:20-22; Luke 8:43-48.

Jesus let her superstition cure her and left her concealment unbroken. Then when the concealed trouble was gone he changed the superstition into belief and built up faith in a fringe into faith in a personal Savior. Our labored explanations of how a purely spiritual teacher could countenance an intensely superstitious belief dissolve immediately as entirely unneeded, when once we understand the unvaryingly affirmative method by which Jesus built upon or built up an existing condition of soul and, in building it up, transformed it.

It is characteristic of the appreciation the evangelist had of Jesus' affirmative way that he starts the story of the anointing at Simon's house at the point where the woman showers tears and kisses upon Jesus' feet and pours out the ointment upon them from the flask. The previous agony of remorse to which the tears point and the forgiveness which Jesus' little parable, spoken to Simon, presupposes have been left unnarrated. Evidently Jesus had given her pardon without severe arraignment of her life, perhaps without even alluding to it. The story even gives us the impression that the woman's penitence and sense of pardon had not been brought out into any open expression before she came to Simon's house. If that be so, anyone who is acquainted with the passional revulsions of feeling which such women sometimes have may recognize such a state of soul as prompting her act of devotion, and may recognize that Jesus then and there was not only showing Simon's own heart to himself but was showing the woman's own heart to herself and was developing her psychological revulsion into true faith.[27]

Luke's gospel is a gospel for women, and it is worth mention, as one more instance of Jesus' method, that when an unnamed woman cried out in a crowd upon the blessedness of being the mother of such a teacher, Jesus did not rebuke the mere expression of delight at a share in the physical production of such a personality. He says not "nay" but "yea." He does not discard the "blessed" but repeats the word and upon the sense of maternal blessedness builds up the idea of the higher ethical blessedness of those who hear the word as he was at that very time speaking it and obey its behests.[28]

It ought to be the study and toil of those who have at heart the saving of their fellow-men and who also believe that the method of Jesus is the right one, to crystallize the affirmative way in which he proceeded into some form of expression which may be easily understood and practically grasped by all. The nearest approach to such an expression which I have been able to find is in Browning's *Paracelsus*. But even that, if it is to express the way of Jesus, needs to be enlarged so as to include not only the intellectual element but the whole inner man and even so, again, the lines are inadequate. Yet I venture to quote them with slight alterations, which the worshipper of Browning will pardon—because they do indicate at least in a general way and along one line the method of Jesus.

---

[27] Luke 7:37-49.   [28] Luke 11:27 f.

There is an inmost center in us all,
Where truth abides in some form; and around
Wall upon wall, the gross flesh hems it in,
This inner, deep perception of the truth;
A baffling and perverting carnal mesh
Blinds it, and makes all error: and, "*to know*"
Rather consists in opening out a way
Whence the imprisoned spendor may escape,
Than in effecting entry for a light
Supposed to be without.[29]

The positive quality of Jesus' work may help us to understand the nature of the *intensity* Jesus directly *demanded* of individuals or actually produced in them. For there is considerable danger of misunderstanding its quality. As the Son of Man, Jesus measured other souls by his own. It cannot be denied that some of the expressions in which he demands intensity of soul wear a hard, forbidding, and even unethical aspect. But we have already seen that in other matters than the one now in hand Jesus did not hestitate to use illustrations from the lives of the unscrupulous, the lazy, the cruel and the fraudulent. It was with similar freedom that he sometimes illustrated the intensity which he required in other souls.

He said on one occasion that no man could be his disciple unless he hated father, mother, wife, children, brothers, sisters, and in fact his own life. The length of the catalogue puts us on the right track. It is simply intended to indicate intensity of soul. If a man actually

---

[29] Browning, *Paracelsus*, I, p. 27.

does hate his father and mother, for example, he in the first place breaks with natural affection, in the second place he seeks to do them injury, or put them out of the way, or leave them altogether. As love is the uniting and blending virtue, so hatred separates and alienates. A man may leave his father or wife in an idle or careless moment. But if he leaves them intensely and violently, it is because he hates them. As Jesus could separate the wickedness of the shrewd steward from his practical foresight, or as he could separate the unscrupulousness of the judge in which he did not resemble God from the yielding to importunity in which he did resemble him, so it seems to have been a perfectly natural process for him to distinguish between the hatred which made a man turn away from his father and mother, and the resolute and determined intensity with which he left them.

The whole utterance, then, is simply a way of expressing, in the intensest language, the corresponding intensity which Jesus required in the hearts of his followers. Just as no one who knew him could for a moment think that he endorsed or even tolerated the fraudulent schemes of the shrewd steward, so no one who knew him could for a moment think that he could counsel a violent breaking of natural ties viewed in and by itself. It was the intensity he aimed at, and the expression served his purpose.

We must even go further and ensphere the intensity with all that gentleness, lowliness of heart, meekness, mercifulness and peace-making spirit which he both required and exhibited. In picturing a loveable character it is all but impossible to avoid a touch of weakness. In picturing a strong character it is all but impossible to avoid a touch of harshness. Jesus did not attempt the impossible. The gentleness he called for, and the peacefulness, were unlimited. So also was the intensity of purpose and consecration. It is this intensity which is now under our eye. Someone asked him in regard to the number of the saved. The question was not a critical one for Jesus. It was individual earnestness that counted. The number of the saved might be few or many. The theoretical question could sleep. The practical one could not. "Strain every nerve," said Jesus, "to enter in at the narrow door." [30]

Jesus also told of a man whose servant came in at evening, tired and jaded with his day's work. His master, however, orders him to prepare his evening meal, serve it, and wait on him till his appetite is fully satisfied, going hungry while he does the work. Even so his master gives him no thanks. Why should he? The man is his slave. He owns him. He might as well thank his fig tree for bearing an extra crop in a good year. The utmost a slave can do and the longest hours he can work are his master's rightful service, just as in the case of his ox or horse. It is not a pleasant story to read or hear, but once more we must remember the way in which Jesus used the story. God was not like the slave-driving owner. Neither were Jesus' disciples related to God as slaves to a slave-driver. But the extra service which the slave had to render was like the extra service

---

[30] Luke 13:23 f.

which the disciple should be ready to render. The
disciples did not work for their Master under compulsion, and their Master was not capable of using such
compulsion. Eliminating the things that must be
eliminated we have the intense service left. For that
the disciples must be ready, making no claim and
seeking no reward.[81]

It is as if he had started with the story of some Sul-
tana whose small and cruel hand compelled her slaves
to shelter her from every chilling wind and who on
occasion ordered them to throw their garments in the
mire, that her dainty feet might go unsoiled. From
such an example of slavery a teacher might turn to
exhort his disciples to be like Shakespeare's lover who
cannot bear to have the wind of heaven visit his be-
loved's face too roughly. Or such a teacher might in-
spire his listeners to be like Raleigh in throwing his
own rich cloak in the mud that Elizabeth's feet might
be protected. The ardent lover and the slave act alike
except in the element of free devotion on the one hand
and physical compulsion on the other.

In reply to the question of a lawyer Jesus told the
parable of the good Samaritan. The lawyer wished to
find out the exact area covered by the word "neighbor" so that when he had gone over it he might stop
the application and exercise of his love. But there was
a previous question which was more important. What
was it to "love with one's whole nature"? It was to
have so full and overflowing a tide of helpfulness and

---

[81] Luke 17:7-10.

compassion in one's soul that it would run every risk and go to every needful expense, present or future, in order to ease the pain and save the life of anyone, no matter who he might be. Such a spirit was the main thing. Opportunities to exercise it would come often enough. Any man who had it would meet them "by chance," whatever the journey on which he was bound. Again we see in Jesus' dealing with the lawyer his persistent demand for broad and rich intensity of soul.

This intensity appears perhaps at its climax in the story which Jesus told Peter about forgiveness. He told the story of a hopelessly and enormously insolvent debtor who, finding his vast obligation forgiven, refused to forgive a fellow servant a most trifling debt. The lord of the great debtor put the unmerciful servant permanently in prison. The severity of the punishment in the story emphasizes the power of forgiveness which Jesus required in the soul of Peter and the other disciples.[32]

Instances and images of the *active service* he required from individuals were almost without number. He did not tell Simon and Andrew to come to him for study, meditation and tuition. He stirred them with the prospect of becoming fishers of men, catching them alive, and keeping them so.[33] The woman of Samaria is sent after her fellow villagers and Peter is given his commission to feed his Master's sheep. Jesus was ready to wear an apron or gird himself with a towel and he

[32] Matt. 18:35.　[33] Mark 1:17; Luke 5:10.

insisted upon similar actual and practical service.[34] Those who were to enter upon his divine propaganda of a kingdom of active service could not wisely take their preparatory tuition while sitting under a Bo tree or even at the place for taking toll. They must rise up from their seats and begin to walk.[35] No doubt the circuits of the twelve and the seventy were necessary for spreading the news of the kingdom. Jesus was the great "peripatetic." He did not walk up and down in the olive grove of his academy. He went about, but he "went about doing good." [36] His pedestrianism always had its objective point. He sought to make each disciple a powerful, tensely strung bow with the arrow notched on the string and drawn resolutely back. There were targets enough in the world. If the arrow were ready and the bow was strung something would appear on every journey. Jesus' followers were not to repress the action of the functions of their being, but to let them find their fullest expression. The place to find that expression was in affirmative service to their fellow men. Jesus aimed at a soundly active soul in a soundly active body. The man he sought to produce and in some cases so nearly succeeded in producing was a man who was richly, totally, positively, affirmatively, constructively, harmoniously, and beneficently active in a single, simple but all comprehending life of "doing good."

---

[34] John 13:6–8.   [35] Mark 2:11.   [36] Acts 10:38.

INDEX